The "WHAT IF" Girl

A Memoir By
Lisa Monks

The *"What If"* Girl
All Rights Reserved
Copyright © 2017 By Lisa Monks

No part of this book may be reproduced in any form or by any electronic or mechanical means, including information storage and retrieval systems, without permission in writing from the author. The only exception is by a reviewer, who may quote short excerpts in a review.

This book is a work of fiction. Names, characters, places, and incidents either are products of the author's imagination or are used fictitiously. Any resemblance to actual persons, living or dead, events, or locales are entirely coincidental.

Cover design by Dottie Scott
Edits by Black Dynasty Publishing
First Edition: July 2017

Contents

- Contents 3
- Foreword 5
- Introduction 8
- Prologue 11
- Chapter One 20
- Chapter Two 30
- Chapter Three 41
- Chapter Four 46
- Chapter Five 66
- Chapter Six 83
- Chapter Seven 99
- Chapter Eight 114
- Chapter Nine 124
- Chapter Ten 136
- Chapter Eleven 156
- Chapter Twelve 188
- Chapter Thirteen 196
- Chapter Fourteen 206
- Chapter Fifteen 225
- Chapter Sixteen 235
- Chapter Seventeen 259
- Chapter Eighteen 266
- Chapter Nineteen 279
- Chapter Twenty 291
- Chapter Twenty-One 319

About THE *Author*.. 325
DEDICATIONS.. 327

FOREWORD
By Michelle Monks and Greg Ioannou

Michelle Monks

We shared a room our entire childhood. To ward off our fear of the dark and stay brave during storms. We would tell stories, sing, or goof around. This created a unique bond between us that forged a foundation for our relationship that would withstand the test of what was to come. There has been joy, like sharing the moment I gave birth to my son; but, there has been great sadness as well. In our mid-teens, our parents would make a move that would forever change both our lives. There was not a joyous outcome, but still it deepened the bond we've had throughout our entire relationship.

We keep in touch constantly, to share stories of our weekly experiences.

I encouraged my sister to write this book, first, because her life did not take the usual expected path to love. It veered off and I believe there are other people out there who need to know there's nothing wrong with that. Secondly, I hoped that she would view herself as courageous and determined in both her battle to find love, but also to find health.

Lastly, I honestly found her stories interesting, entertaining, and enlightening. After years of hearing them, it was time to share those stories with the rest of the world.

This book has been challenging, trust me. It wasn't easy to constantly harass her for six years to write it. There was a lot of swearing and telling me to stop fucking bugging her to write a book. She's not a writer. Frankly, I'm not sure what possessed me to continue pushing her. Most people would've said fuck it, don't write it then.

There have been many ups and downs in her pursuit to get this done, but it's been an honor to be part of the journey.

It's like a grown-up version of those two little girls that shared stories to keep from being taken by the boogeyman under the bed.

And well, basically, I won the argument. It might've taken me six years, but I got her to do it.

As sisters, we have an unbreakable bond.

***

Greg Ioannou

I was introduced to Lisa Monks by an editor friend in January 2012. Lisa had written a hot tell-all memoir called *I Lost My Boyfriend to Dolce&Gabbana Perfume* and had been trying to find a publisher for it. I read it and realized that it was a fantastic story -- but ... wow!

I Lost My Boyfriend named names, said exactly who had treated her well and who had treated her like dirt, with lots and lots and lots of details. Would I like to publish it?

YES! Could I publish it? No -- I'd have spent the rest of my life fighting lawsuits.

Lisa came to my office and started telling me some of the stories that weren't in the book, and they were even steamier that what she'd written about. We talked about different ways of presenting the material, how to focus it in different ways.

Over the next few months, Lisa tried two other approaches: a "nice" version which only talked about the people who had treated her well, and a hot, 50 Shades treatment that was the raunchiest version yet.

Because of the number of sports figures in the book, at one point we renamed it *Players*. Another version was called *Ball Players*. Clever, but not subtle, that one.

Around the same time, Lisa worked on a movie proposal for the story.

Although the presentation evolved, the story at its core didn't. Her very first email to me nailed it: "I have a book with important advice, as well as compassion for people who struggle with loneliness, and the self-destructive behavior that it can lead to. I share my life experience, in hopes to comfort those who've been through the same, and to forewarn those that are headed down the same path."

The book has evolved over the years. It is still a memoir, but it is now fictionalized -- the names have all been changed, and details of the stories have been changed so that it is no longer possible to identify some of the people in her life. But the life lessons are the same.

Come meet The "What If" Girl…

INTRODUCTION

What if everyone you loved cheated on you?
What if everyone who loved you left you?
What if every one of them came back to you, years later, begging for you to give them another chance, to love them with all your heart the way you loved them back then?
What if you didn't do what you did in the first place and you just loved me the right way, the first time?
What if you treated me then like you say you will now?
What if you would have realized what you had, while you had me?

I guess that's why I call myself, The "What if" Girl.

I remember when we met and you asked me to jump off that cliff with you. I was young, naïve, and scared. But then, I became fearless, because I trusted you with all my heart.
So, I ran and leapt off that rock with your hand in mine, but when my foot left the ground, I looked back and you had let go.
You didn't jump at all.
You protected yourself and stayed where you were. Safe. While I plunged deep into waters unknown.
Now, twenty years later, all four of you have come back, and you want me to feel the way I felt back then.
Only I don't.

I can tell you want me to pretend. Wouldn't that be nice, I think to myself, to be cherished, and loved so dearly?
You say you would treat me like a Queen.
Would you really?
Maybe the truth is you haven't changed at all.

Maybe it would all turn out like it did the first time. I know what I want, I know what I deserve., I won't settle for less this time, because if I learned anything from the four of you coming back, it's that I'm worth it...

Prologue
Abort Mission

What if I don't make it?

Pull it together Lily, I said to myself.

I can't afford to miss this appointment. I can't speed and risk being pulled over. I can't believe I slept in. I never sleep through my alarm. I don't even miss a hair appointment for Christ's sake, never mind something as important as this.

As I was speeding down the highway out of control, weaving in and out of traffic, I cut a guy off. Of course, he laid on his horn and I gave him the finger in response. I had to make it into the city and I didn't have time to be stuck behind a slow driver like him.

My whole body was shaking as I was driving. I tried to dig through my purse for some Tylenol to ease my pounding headache, but gave up when I almost swerved into the next lane again.

Fuck! Why is everything so difficult?

One by one, I had picked up and whipped the entire contents of my purse onto the car floor as I frantically dug through it for some fucking Tylenol, still not finding any. I looked up and noticed it was my exit, reeled my car over into the far-right lane and pulled onto the Allen Road Expressway, southbound ramp; there was no time to stop just for a few pills.

Holding in my urge to vomit and cry, I raced through the city streets of Toronto to make it to my destination. I felt so sick I could barely focus on the road and I was terrified that I was going to be late. I didn't know if they'd still take me if I was late.

Thank God, it was spring and I didn't have a snow storm to contend with. I had to make it in time; I would not be able to live another week feeling like this.

Do other grown women get themselves into this predicament or was I a special kind of fuck up? Were extremely long periods of loneliness a legitimate excuse for such reckless behavior? Does anyone else feel the way I feel about being single for years? Am I the only one making bad decisions due to loneliness?

I believe so. I was starting to believe I was the only

person in the world that would accept that excuse or even understand it.

When I reached downtown, I looked for the closest parking lot, parked my car, flung open the door and threw up on the pavement. It was embarrassing and humiliating, even without a single soul in sight.

I rummaged through my glove box for something to wipe my mouth with, emptying most of its contents onto the floor, doubling the mess that I had made from my purse.

Great! Now I had an even bigger mess to clean up.

As much as it bugged me to leave it there, I would have to deal with that later.

Finally, I found some napkins, courtesy of Starbucks, wiped my mouth then quickly headed toward the drab, gray-colored building. I pushed the buzzer and after a moment, a woman's voice with a strong nasal pitch came through on the tiny intercom.

"Name?" asked the voice.

My head was pounding which made the sound of her voice ring through my ears like nails on a chalkboard. While gagging back the remaining bile in my stomach and fighting the overpowering urge to vomit yet again, I managed to reply, "Lily Monroe."

I heard the loud noise of a buzzer all around me as the small gate slid open, revealing a long hallway with a door at the other end.

It was comforting to know this institution was just as hard to get into as a maximum-security prison and I didn't have to worry about being seen there.

Once inside, I tried my best to maintain eye contact with the floor to hide my feelings of shame. When I came up to the front desk, I matched up the nasal voice to a gloomy looking receptionist. She was in her late fifties with large rimmed glasses and short, tightly curled, gray hair. She looked like one of those frighteningly stern nurses you'd see in a black and white horror film, which seemed fitting given the circumstances I was in.

She handed me forms to fill out and I slowly made my way into the waiting area and sat down.

There was a question on the form that I had to answer about my certainty going through with this procedure. As horrible as this sounds, I wrote, *I feel so sick, I can't wait to get this over with.*

Even though the famous athlete I was with wanted this baby, I did not. In fact, I was certain I did not ever want children. There I said it, the unthinkable, the socially unacceptable declaration a woman isn't allowed to make.

Why is there so much pressure to get married and have kids? Why are women still judged for seeking casual, physical comfort and intimacy from a man during long periods of being single? I was sick of having this argument with the world; moreover, not wanting kids had nothing to do with my age. Raising another human being and guaranteeing that I can create nothing but happiness, health, and an easy life for that child is something that I take very seriously. I also wanted to be sure that the child would have a mother who had her shit together. At this point in my life, I was far from that.

What made me even more sure of this decision was that it was making me so sick I could not function as a human being. I couldn't work. I had to support myself. I had bills to pay. I had no choice.

Sure, after giving birth and possibly taking a DNA test, I'd be set for life, financially that is, but that's not the kind of person I am. He made it quite clear that he was not ready to make a commitment to me; yet, he was still not happy about my decision to not keep this baby. I never saw or heard from him again after I told him that I wasn't going through with having his child. I had no doubt in my mind that this was the right thing to do, especially since I didn't even think it was possible for me to get pregnant at the age of forty.

I had to terminate this pregnancy.

It's the worst experience to share with a room full of strangers, even though we were all in the same situation. No one wanted to look at anyone. The feelings of shame, guilt, and uncertainty were palpable in the air. I tried not to look around the room out of respect for personal privacy.

However, I did manage to notice that everyone had someone with them, except me.

As I sat in the waiting room, with my hands over my mouth because the urge to vomit never went away, the receptionist kept looking over at me. I thought to myself, she must have seen this type of thing before; yet, a feeling of paranoia quickly crept into my mind.

Did she know something I didn't?

Was my constant, intense nausea abnormal?

Why doesn't anyone else look like they are feeling as sick as I am?

After an hour or more had passed, the receptionist got up and headed toward me.

"Excuse me, Miss. I've noticed that you are here by yourself. They won't allow you to go through with the operation unless someone is picking you up."

I slowly looked up at her and forced out the words,

"Yes, I know. My boyfriend is at work; he is picking me up as soon as it's over."

The receptionist gave me a suspicious look that said she saw right through me, but luckily, she didn't push it, she just took my paperwork and sat back down at her desk.

Since the man who put me in this situation wasn't returning my calls he obviously wasn't going to be picking me up and I was too ashamed to tell my family, so they were out of the equation as well. Only my girlfriend, Christine, knew I was here and she didn't drive.

*** ***

After being released, I stopped for a bagel at the closest coffee shop. I hadn't eaten in days since the nausea was so intense. I could finally hold down solid food, what a relief.

I got back into my car, lied down, and slept for hours. I was at the lowest point in my life.

How did I get here? My obsession with finding true love was destroying me.

I believe a woman's value as a mate comes from her integrity as a human being. A relationship should be based on how good of a match you think you are for each other. Not thrown away due to how early a woman gives in to having sex with you, but society was fighting me all the way. My belief system was leading me down the wrong path.

Is this what they call a midlife crisis?

I was going to have to reinvent myself, things had to change. My life had to get on track. Heck, Madonna came from nothing and is one of the most successful business women I know, she's reinvented herself countless times, each one being just as successful as the last. There must be at least one version of Lily Monroe that equals success.

I had two college degrees and an acting agent.

A promising future, I thought.

I was so innocent growing up, until I started partying and became lonely. Alcohol mixed with loneliness brought out a careless, reckless, and destructive side of me.

The most important things I learned from my mother were that: *You have the freedom to make your own decisions, but you better have the strength to support them.* And: *Women are not second-class citizens, nor inferior, to men.*

The lessons I learned, didn't learn, and the crazy experiences that I've had over the years, I wish to share with you in the hopes of giving comfort, entertainment, and strength to other people who can relate to my stories. Welcome to the life of Lily Monroe…

Chapter One
Georgetown Boys

Let me start at the beginning. The year is 1980. I'm an attractive twelve-year-old girl with long brown hair, natural blonde highlights from summers spent swimming and tanning in the sun, green eyes, and a killer smile that lights up any room as soon as I step through the door, so I'm told. Without high heels, I stand at five feet five inches tall; my body type, sporty and curvy. In a nutshell, I'm easy on the eyes.

I grew up in Georgetown, Ontario. Which is situated on the Credit River, located approximately sixty kilometers west of Toronto with a population, at the time, of seventeen thousand people.

Georgetown was your typical run-of-the-mill, small town. On every street corner, each building essentially looked the same with plenty of exposed bricks. Everyone in Georgetown was heavily into sports. You either spent your time playing or watching them, or both. In the winter, our town held an annual Bantam Hockey Tournament at the local arena. The best teams from across North America attended this tournament, including boys aged twelve to thirteen years old.

This is where my attraction to fit, athletic boys began. I started young, looking for my one true love.

My friends and I would spend our weekends at the arena, watching all the hockey games, hoping to meet cute boys.

The teams playing on this day were the Georgetown Raiders versus the Waterloo Wolves.

As I sat in the stands watching the game, I noticed an attractive young man from the home team making passes at me every time he skated by. He looked taller than me, maybe five foot nine inches tall with thick, brown, wavy hair that fell just below the nape of his neck. It was obvious he worked out, judging by his well-built body and his nice, tight, round bum. His eyes were a deep blue. I would lose myself in his gaze every time he stared at me. Last but not least were his full luscious lips that looked so kissable.

My friends and I stayed until the game was over, which seemed to go on forever. It had constant action and drama. In the first period, one of the spectators was hit in the head with a puck, split his forehead open and blood gushed out everywhere. The game was postponed until first aid attendants arrived and carried the young man off in a stretcher. There was no score in the third period, there were two guys in the penalty box at the same time, and at one point the goalie was removed for a power play. There was one minute left in the game, and we were looking at overtime. At this point, I no longer cared who won; my only concerns were that my curfew was getting closer and how was I going to run into this cute boy I was crushing on.

I waited in the foyer after the game, hoping to see him. As soon as our eyes met I could feel an instant connection. It is strange how you can instantly like a perfect stranger. Some people we are destined to meet.

He walked right up to me and said, "Hi. My name is Greg. What's yours?"

"Lily," I replied.

"That's a pretty name. Do you mind if I walk you home?"

"Okay," I said, a bit overly enthusiastic.

As we got outside and started walking, I noticed he

wasn't carrying any hockey gear and to make light conversation, I asked, "So, where is your hockey equipment?"

"Huh? I left my bag with my parents. So, what school do you go to?"

"Georgetown Essex. How about you?"

"Georgetown Tech. I'm from Acton originally and just moved here about a month ago," he replied.

We continued walking down the street. I was vibrating with excitement. I'd never felt this before. This was my first real crush. I was nervous and thrilled at the same time.

When we reached the bottom of my street there was a long awkward silence, until finally he made a move.

"So, a pretty girl like you must have a boyfriend?"

"No one special right now," I replied.

"Really," he moved in closer and pulled my hips into his, my heart was pounding.

I closed my eyes and that's when he planted the first kiss.

My first kiss.

His lips were soft, our kisses felt innocent and gentle. From that moment on, we tried to run into each other after every one of his hockey games. We spent most of our time making out.

See, at the age of twelve, Mother Nature had blessed me with the curves of a grown woman, which made every young man's penis stand at attention with one glance. Something I had no idea of at the time. The downside to my early blooming was I did not have the sexual desire to go with it. My mind was still the mind of an innocent girl. Holding hands and kissing was as far as my curiosity went. Every time I was with Greg, I felt like a goalie during practice, trying to fend off all the shots from his teammates. Greg kept trying to go up my top and I would block him, then he'd try to go down my pants, and I'd block him there as well. It was up then down, then up, then down with him. I had no experience on defense.

I was quite shy and confused as to why kissing wasn't enough. Neither I nor any of my close friends were even curious about sex or a boy's penis. He kept trying to go further but I wasn't ready for that. Thank God for curfews. So far, that's how I'd managed to escape his advances every night. As this power struggle continued, and he realized I wasn't ready to go further, I started to see him less. He used hockey as an excuse, the very thing that brought us together. I was twelve and naïve. I believed him, it bothered me, but I had no idea he was playing me. This theme followed me throughout my life. Men wanting me to do sexual things I was neither interested in, nor ready for.

A few months later, while I'm lying in my bedroom, the phone rings. It was my high school friend, Maria.

"Lily, there's something important I have to tell you."

As soon as I heard those words come out of her mouth, my stomach did a flip, and I felt sick. I knew the news wasn't going to be good. I almost didn't want Maria to tell me what was going on but my curiosity got the best of me.

"Maria, what is it?"

"You know Greg, that guy you are seeing? Rumor has it, he already has a girlfriend from his hometown, Acton."

"Really, are you sure?" I replied.

"It's true. I heard she is a real bitch too. One of my classmates from gym class is friends with her and said she came all the way from Acton just to chew Greg out for cheating on her."

I sat up with a frown on my face, "How did she know Greg was cheating?"

"Well, when my friend told me that she was

hanging out with her girlfriend and a guy named Greg from Acton, who is her friend's boyfriend, I asked what he looked like. I put two and two together, realized it was the same guy, and let it slip. I'm so sorry, Lily. I didn't do it on purpose, honest."

"I can't believe you told her that," I replied angrily.

"No. Well, yes. I mean I thought she had a right to know. I didn't want her to find out I knew and didn't tell her. She'd come after me and kick my ass," she said.

I sighed, "Is there anything else I should know?"

"No Lily, I swear! Well there is. She asked for your number and said she was going to call you. That's why I called you first, I wanted to warn you. I'm so sorry I was the one that had to tell you all this. I wish it wasn't true but it is," said Maria.

"It's okay Maria, thanks for telling me."

"Are you all right, Lily?"

"Yep, I'll be just fine. I gotta go. Thanks for giving me the heads-up, bye," I hung up the phone without allowing Maria to say goodbye.

The truth is, I knew the floodgates were about to open. She would be able to tell that I was bawling my eyes out and I didn't want her to know how hurt I was. I felt sick to my stomach. I wanted to throw up, but sometimes when we are hurting we pretend as if nothing matters; to avoid giving others the satisfaction of knowing we've been destroyed. I was so upset I was shaking. Greg was my first real crush, who lied to me and stole my first real kiss.

It felt awful. I couldn't believe I was so stupid. Greg was the guy I had pledged my virginity to because I thought we had something special.

What a fool I was.

What am I supposed to do if I can't trust my own heart? It had just disappointed me for the very first time.

As I sat there in silence, feeling sorry for myself, the telephone rang. I did not want to answer it, dreading it was Greg, or worse, Greg's angry girlfriend, but I found some courage and answered it anyway. After all, as far as I was concerned, I was his angry girlfriend and had a right to be pissed about him cheating on me.

"Hello."

A female voice barked through the line, "Who the hell is this? Are you Lily?"

"Yes. This is Lily," I answered.

"My name is Jenny, Greg's girlfriend. Do you normally steal other guys from their girlfriends?"

I sat there in silence as tears began to swell up in my eyes and pour down my cheeks.

"Go on chicken shit, get on the phone and tell her you already have a girlfriend."

I wanted it to be a lie, just a mean jealous girl prank, but then I faintly heard Greg's voice in the background as the bitch was yelling at him to get on the phone. My heart sank. I felt even more sick.

Is this what love was going to feel like?

"If I ever find out that you are still seeing Greg, I swear to God, I'm going to come straight to your house and scratch your eyes out! You hear me?" screamed Jenny before she slammed down the phone.

I sat there in silence as I wiped the tears from my eyes.

The sick feeling in my stomach had now changed to dread and fear, especially at the thought of running into him in public. I got under my comforter and began to cry. I didn't want to face the world or talk to anyone.

Just as I was in the middle of my pity party and bawling my eyes out, there was a knock at my bedroom door.

"What is it?" I barked.

"Lily, can you come downstairs? Your father and I want to have a family meeting," my mother's voice came through the door.

Their timing couldn't have been worse, now I must go face my family at the worst moment of my life.

I got out of bed, looked in the mirror, wiped the tears from my eyes, and slowly wandered downstairs to the living room. My only thought was that I could not wait for this day to end.

Chapter Two
Harsh Reality

Upon entering the living room, my entire family was already seated on the fuzzy, purple sofa, staring right at me as if I was some sort of alien. Considering what I just went through, a family meeting was not on the top of my list of fun things to do right now.

Before I continue, I feel it's only fair to tell you a bit about my family.

First, we have my father. At age forty-two, he still had his full head of thick, black hair that was always slicked back with a bit of gel. He had brown eyes, in fact, everyone in my family had *shit brown* eyes as we called them. Except me, my eyes were green or hazel depending on the day. Whenever my dad smiled, you couldn't help but notice the big gap between his two front teeth. He always told us that it was a sign of superior intelligence. He was the quintessential strong and silent type; rarely voicing any opinion unless it was necessary. His easy going, laid-back attitude made it so my mother did all the disciplining and worrying about money and bills. She was the responsible one. My dad was the dreamer.

My mother was of Ukrainian descent, measuring five foot three inches tall. She was an honest, straight forward, no bullshit, ethical woman with a heart of gold, if you earned it. Her naturally wavy brown hair was kept short. She wasn't one to fuss with her appearance after having children. Her focus and drive was to provide for her family and save for a comfortable retirement. Her clothing preference was loose and comfortable. She often dressed in jeans or black dress pants paired with a blouse or t-shirt.

To my right was my fifteen-year-old sister, Layla. Five feet seven inches tall with brown eyes and beautiful, flowing, long, naturally wavy hair. My older sister often referred to me as a 'spoiled brat' at the time. Layla enjoyed arguing and being bossy, and was annoyed by the special treatment I got, that came with being the youngest in the family. She would often loan my clothes to her friends, who couldn't even fit them. My favorite and only pair of blue jeans were returned ruined after she let a girl, twice my size, wear them; yet, Layla's clothes were completely off limits.

We shared a room and were close when we were little, but I didn't spend much time with Layla once she reached her teen years, since she went to a different school and was either working, swimming, or out with her boyfriend.

Lynn was the oldest sister in my family. Age nineteen, also five feet seven inches tall, she had shoulder length, super curly, dark brown hair that looked like an afro some days. Lynn always stayed in shape, her muscular body and wild party girl personality brought around many male suitors on a regular basis. Her choice of clothes was mostly low-rise bell-bottom jeans, and tight-cropped t-shirts.

First, she got caught with marijuana and birth control pills at the age of sixteen. Then, she got in trouble for some burnt knives I found in my Barbie case. It wasn't my fault that I brought the burnt knives to my mom when I found them, I had no idea what *hot knifing hash* was at the time. Lynn was out of control, but brought home straight A's, this was her constant defense for her delinquent behavior. When she finished high school, she immediately went off to university to study psychology.

My sisters were always getting in shit for staying out past curfew and for not helping with the chores. My mom, while she was fuming, would make me sit at the kitchen table as she waited for them to get home. Usually Layla was the worst culprit for staying out late. I always told my mom I didn't want to ever upset her the way my sisters did, and I was never going to be like them. Looking back now, I can see why my sisters thought I was annoying, with my *Miss goody two shoes* attitude.

After getting the evil eye from my entire family for taking so long to arrive in the living room, I finally sat down on the armchair waiting for the procession to begin.

"It pains me to tell you all this, but I have just been let go at the post office. My five-year contract was up for renewal and they decided to hire someone else. Now, your mother and I have discussed this for quite a long time and we have both agreed that it's time to move out of Georgetown," said my father.

"Why? Can't you just find another job here?" I asked.

"Sweetie, it's not as easy as that," replied my father.

"Why not?" Layla asked.

"Your mother and I have given this a lot of thought.

We're not getting any younger and in a few years, we should be considering retirement. As it stands now, we can barely pay the property tax on this house," he replied.

"Layla and I will both get jobs to help," I said.

"No. We're moving to Huntsville, end of discussion."

"Huntsville? Where the fuck is Huntsville?" yelled Layla.

"Watch your language, missy," my mother glared at her.

"We decided to purchase a gas station with a convenience store attached. At least this way we don't have to work for someone else. Everyone always needs gas," said my father in a very *matter of fact* tone.

Looking back, I completely understand their motivation for wanting to work for themselves. In our modern times, during a full-blown recession, when holding down a full-time job is considered a luxury, being able to have the freedom to be your own boss and not having to answer to anyone is something that I deeply respect now. My father always had issues with authority figures and believed in getting things done on his own terms so it seemed natural that he would be his own boss.

At the end of the conversation, Layla, Lynn, and I

were told we had less than two weeks before the big move. I loved our house in Georgetown. It was three stories tall and sat at the top of a hill near a basketball court. We had a front and back yard with a seven-foot-long, gray, brick wall, covered in green vines and beautiful morning glories. It surrounded our twenty-by-forty foot, heated, in-ground swimming pool. Behind the brick fence, we had a horseshoe pit and a garden where my mom grew fresh vegetables.

We were happy in Georgetown. We stayed slim and fit from our swimming pool. Hell, I lost weight just from walking a mile and a half to and from school every day. My family was not blessed with fast metabolism genes, so having an active life was important.

What I was going to miss most were our frequent family barbeques and pool parties. My life in Georgetown consisted of swimming in our pool, working on my tan, hanging out with friends, and biking to the convenience store.

For my last two weeks, I spent as much time with my friends as possible, skipping school, since I was moving and hanging with the wrong crowd.

When it was time to leave, I said all my good-byes with plenty of tears, and left Georgetown with a heavy heart. My father had this crazy idea that getting everyone fast food through the takeout window at Wendy's before getting on the highway was going to make everything better. I shrank down in the back seat, pouted, and refused to order anything. Like fast food was going to help make this day any better. My Dad wasn't one to dwell on things. He shrugged, put everyone else's order in, and off we went.

As we arrived at our new home in Huntsville, I was in utter shock. The front exterior of the house was covered in snow colored, wooden planks that served as the walls for this hideous structure. The roof was shaped like an isosceles triangle in the glamorous color of monochrome, alpine brown. Overall, it had the look of one of those worn-down cabins in the woods.

The house was semi-detached from the grocery store my parents purchased, known as *The Lucky Dollar* Super Market, roughly the same dimensions as most convenience stores. Two gas pumps were erected outside, that looked so ancient you'd swear it was there since the land before time. *The Lucky Dollar* sign was barely attached to the roof and looked like it was about to fall off any minute.

How were we going to thrive here? Only God knows.

As our car drove through the side driveway, I noticed two large white containers that held bags of ice for the customers to purchase. On the complete opposite side of the building was where you could gain entrance to our new home.

Inside wasn't much better.

It contained only one floor; one hallway that led to all three bedrooms, a living room, an ugly narrow kitchen with old, warped, off-white countertops, and one small bathroom full of black mold. It was gross.

Everything in this house was old, cheap, ugly, and outdated. Lynn was lucky she was off to university in a few days where she was going to live in residence. She didn't have to stay in this hell hole.

No matter how hard I tried, I was miserable up there. My nice long walks to school had now turned into a long bus ride to school, full of kids that stank like stale lunchmeat. I remember my first day at my new high school. Layla and I were in the guidance counselor's office choosing classes and everyone was staring at us as they walked by. I felt like an animal in a cage. All the students knew each other from birth and we were the outsiders. Their idea of fun was snowmobile races, smash up derbys, cruising the back roads, drinking beer and smoking pot, which I eventually joined in on, and became accustomed to. Although I never felt like I quite fit in there.

Where was my group? The cool kids that played sports, dieted, dressed fashionably, dropped acid before French class, because if the teacher made us do that stupid duck dance or watch that dumb French clown show one more time I was going to snap.

In Huntsville, there was not a care in the world of what was trending in the fashion industry. The main high school cliques were the beer-drinking potheads who ditched class, the academics, and the thespians. Whenever I got close to making a new girlfriend, they would get a boyfriend, then disappear from my life completely, forcing me to drift between each group. In the end, I never felt like I was one of them, and just made friends when I could.

After living up in Huntsville for a few months, I went back to visit my friends in Georgetown. The looks on their faces were priceless after I drank a beer. I wondered why everyone was looking at me weird. Oh, my God, I had just shotgunned a beer; no other teenage girl in Georgetown was drinking like that.

Who was I?

It was at that moment I realized I didn't fit in back in Georgetown. I was slowly morphing into a northern girl, whatever that was. Great, now I don't fit in anywhere!

What I missed most was my outdoor life in Georgetown. I had no desire to be outside in Huntsville because the bugs were atrocious. We had black fly season, during which if you even stepped outside for a minute the flies were so thick they would fly in your mouth, ears, eyes, and up your nose. Then we had mosquito season, they kept you up all night with that buzzing sound they make, even if it was just that one you couldn't find and kill. Turn the lights on and he disappears, turn it off and try to go back to sleep and the buzzing starts all over again. After that was deer and horse fly season, their bites left a welt the size of a silver dollar.

I couldn't go from swimming in my own clear pool, which I could see the bottom in, to swimming in a lake that was so dark you couldn't see a damn thing. Who knows what lurked below?

The only entertainment I was left with was the unique experience of sleepovers in friends' houses that were heated by a wood stove, which is freezing in the morning when it's the middle of winter and it's twenty below because the fire dies at some point in the night while everyone's asleep. When you crawl out from under the duvet in the morning and put your bare feet on the floor, it's like stepping onto an ice rink. That woke me up quick; there was no need for caffeine for a pick-me-up in the morning up north.

I was deeply depressed over moving to Huntsville and never got over it. I never formed the close connections I had with my girlfriends in Georgetown, and I never gained the popularity I had left behind. I quickly lost interest in school and sports. My new interests were partying, drinking, and smoking pot. Luckily, I got sick of pot real fast, by the time I was in grade ten to be exact because it was making me fat and tired. Partying led to midnight binges and my friends always had the best food.

All we did was cruise the back roads, push each other's cars out of snow banks, go to dances above arenas, and drink. I couldn't wait to grow up so I could move back to the city. What I didn't know was that my wish was about to come true.

CHAPTER THREE
Orgy Town

In some respects, I was extremely lucky my family moved to Huntsville. Take for example the town's lack of fashionable clothing stores. It was this exact point that inspired me to go to college to study business related to fashion, which meant finally moving back to civilization.

Off I went to Seneca College, I was eighteen years old and boarding with a middle-aged, Filipino couple. It was a three-level townhouse and far superior to my parent's place. I had my own room on the top floor and full access to the basement, which I always had to myself for studying. I was within walking distance to my college campus, and couldn't have asked for a more perfect place to live.

The only rules of the house were that my boyfriend, Jamie, could come over and stay as late as he wanted, but wasn't allowed to sleep overnight, perfect.

I met Jamie in my last year of high school at one of the infamous arena dances in Huntsville. He was five foot eleven, blue eyed, cute, nice smile with white teeth, friendly, thick, curly, brown hair, very kind personality, and smart. He was a great guy. I never once saw him look at any other women or flirt with them.

The night we first met, he wore a light blue cotton shirt which was purposely unbuttoned to show off his sexy six-pack. He walked up to me and asked me to dance. As strange as this might sound, back then if you kissed someone you were automatically a couple.

We finished up high school and both of us started college at Seneca, but on different campuses. All I did for two years was study, study, and more studying. I even studied in his bedroom while Jamie was having a party downstairs at his house. It didn't make me popular but I didn't care. I started getting amazing grades, learned a lot, and found out I wasn't as stupid and slow like I'd been treated by my teachers and family in the past. This was a new start for me that set me on a path to discover my potential and was endlessly more satisfying than getting drunk.

One morning as I'm doing my laundry in the basement, Myla, the wife of the Filipino couple, came downstairs.

"Doing your laundry before the weekend so you can see Jamie?"

"I'm just doing my laundry," I said.

"Oh. I see."

She stood there for a few moments, in absolute silence, before uttering, "You know Lily, if you want to share my husband that's okay by me."

I immediately turned around and gave her a discomforting look. Within lightning speed, my current residence had turned from a dream home to a nightmarish hell. I was eighteen and had a boyfriend. Why the hell would I want to hook up with an old, married man? I certainly don't recall any wording on my lease, stating a requirement to sleep with the landlord's husband. For the sake of my studies I just pretended the incident never happened and said nothing to Myla as she wobbled herself back upstairs.

The next day, I tried my best to keep this awkward situation out of my mind. After a while I couldn't stand it anymore so I contacted the only person I could think of who would understand, Jamie. All I wanted was a man by my side, who was in my same age group, as I studied for school.

Perhaps, I was a bit overly paranoid at the time but I had no idea what kind of people my landlords were and what they were capable of and I had no intention of wanting to find out. Jamie was my knight in shining armor. He rushed as fast as he could to my rescue. As soon as he arrived, I gave him the deepest kiss I could muster, which I think surprised him. After that, all I did was study in my room for my midterm that was coming up.

It was only midnight when the phone started ringing off the hook.

I was curious as to why the landlords weren't answering it.

The telephone kept ringing, then it would stop and then it would start again. After over ten minutes of this I couldn't concentrate on my books to study so I finally got up and went downstairs to answer the phone. It was my mother, hysterical on the other end of the phone. She was freaking out at me because I was being kicked out of the couple's home by the end of the week. The reason they gave my mom was that they claimed Jamie slept overnight which was against the rules. I told my mom that their reason was false. I had followed all the rules except the one that meant me sleeping with her frumpy, unattractive husband.

The smell of pot was billowing out of the bottom of their bedroom door that night too.

I packed up all my belongings on what ended up being my nineteenth birthday and went to live with my Aunt Rose and cousin Marie in Mississauga. My school was in North York, which meant a much longer commute, but at least I was safe and out of harm's way.

Chapter Four
Hollywood North

After graduating college and before applying my newfound skills in the fashion world, I moved back up north to be with my parents and started looking for a job there. I heard Deerhurst Resort was hiring, so I dropped off a résumé and a few days later, I got the job. As soon as I paid off my college debt, and saved enough money my plan was to move back to the city.

Deerhurst is a picturesque cottage country-styled resort in Huntsville, located on the lake. The grounds are surrounded by acres of lush green trees of all types, shapes and sizes. Onsite amenities include golfing, skiing, water sports, tennis, a nightclub, and a Vegas styled show.

The dining room had an upscale rustic feel with polished, chestnut colored, hardwood floors and exposed brick along each pillar that looked almost like pebbles you would find on a beach. The roof was a circular gazebo type of design in a darker chestnut shade made entirely of wood. Each table seated no less than ten people with five chairs on either side. Each chair had its own unique design, consisting of a wooden frame with a burgundy or emerald green colored cushion in a paisley pattern. The table was dressed with individual placemats that had a gold undertone, topped with cream-colored napkins which were carefully folded in the shape of a pyramid and positioned at each place setting. The most stunning attractions in the room were the floor-to-ceiling glass windows where guests could admire the stunning view of the lake while they had a five-star dining experience.

    I worked at the front office, performing mundane tasks eight hours a day, five days a week. The pay was not exactly great but I stuck it out. One of my tasks involved cashing out all the servers at the end of their shift. I quickly learned that servers were making twice the amount of money than I did and only worked half the amount of time. Instead of feeling sorry for myself, during one of my breaks when the dining room was quiet, I spoke to the head maître d' about wanting to become a server.

    "Do you have any serving experience," he asked.

    "No, but I am a fast learner."

He gave me a quick glance over, checking out my entire body, "Follow me."

He walked me over to the head waitress of the ballroom. The same ballroom where the nightly Vegas shows were held.

"Kim, this Lily. She's interested in becoming a cocktail waitress. Would you mind giving her the lowdown on waitressing?"

"No problem," Kim eagerly replied.

I started practicing by carrying a tray with glasses full of water when the ballroom was empty, for a few nights a week. Eventually she taught me the basics of how to present the bill, which is a complete art form to maximize your chances of receiving good tips. When Kim finally thought that I was ready, she put me on the floor to be a cocktail waitress for the Vegas show. I did extremely well and quit my front office position to start my first waitressing job.

Kim and I got along very well and soon became best friends. She had a very sexy nineteen eighties look with long auburn hair that seemed to always stay perfectly in place. Her face was almost doll-like with minimal black eye shadow, rosy cheeks, light pink colored lipstick, brown eyes, and an hourglass figure. I understood why Kim was the head waitress. What I think most people liked about her was the feeling you could tell her anything without the worry of her blabbing it to the world. Besides, her fun upbeat personality was extremely contagious.

My first confession to Kim was my feelings toward Jamie. When I first got the job at Deerhurst, Jamie ran off to his annual tree planting job that he got through his family connections. I hated it when he'd go during college break because he was gone for several months every spring and summer. Jamie always wrote me love letters from the woods on a piece of tree bark. Back then, we didn't have email, and though his gesture was sweet and romantic, it still didn't make up for lost time. Now, after graduating from college, Jamie still went to his summer job; despite my best efforts begging him not to go. I knew if he went for a third time, we were going to grow apart.

I told Kim that I was starting to fall out of love with Jamie. He was my first real boyfriend, and my family loved him to death, it killed me to admit it, but I knew it was time to move on. Since Jamie was in the middle of the woods, that also meant no access to a telephone, so only Kim and I knew my secret.

After finishing the night shift at the Vegas show, I went home to my room and couldn't get to sleep. Not having my boyfriend to cuddle with was starting to drive me crazy. To kill the time, I would watch television 'til three in the morning.

On one night, *Funny Girl* was playing. Based on a true story, Barbra Streisand plays the comedian, Fanny Brice, alongside Omar Sharif who plays Nick Arnstein, a professional gambler and con artist with gentlemanly charms and good manners. Taking place in the nineteen twenties, the story is about how Fanny desperately wanted to join the Ziegfeld Follies as a chorus girl and to eventually become a big star. Back then, the Ziegfeld Follies were the equivalent of today's Broadway musicals with a dash of high-class Vaudeville variety show. Styling is often held at lavish venues mimicking the feel of a grand palace. Fanny lived in the Jewish slums of the Lower East Side of New York, which I related to my life, growing up in that shithole house attached to The Lucky Dollar supermarket. Fanny was a shy, awkwardly beautiful woman with occasional sassy and quick dry wit, just like me.

As the story progresses, Fanny and Nick get married and move into a luxurious mansion where Fanny gives birth to a daughter. Nick eventually begins to lose heavily at the gaming tables and everything he tries in life, ends in failure. Fanny continues to be successful on stage and Nick starts to resent her and places his interests and needs above hers, causing the marriage to collapse. This immediately made me think of my current relationship with Jamie and how we were gradually falling apart. I respect the fact that he had a job to go to but having no time together for five months was not acceptable in my books. Every time he would come back from his tree planting job, we had several moments of awkward silence. As I watched Funny Girl it felt like I was seeing a parallel version of my own life on the TV screen.

Toward the end of the film, Nick gets involved in a shady bond scheme which sends him to prison for two years. The ending involves Nick coming to Fanny's dressing room before her performance and tells Fanny goodbye. Barbra Streisand then sings the final song of the picture entitled 'My Man'. The way she carries herself, taking responsibility for her choices and showing that she will go on with her life; despite, what's happened to her, is what truly inspired me and rang true for my own life.

As I sat there in bed, watching the end credits roll, the tears began to fall down my cheeks like rain drops on a stormy night. Something was missing in my life, a purpose. Deep down, I knew a career in the fashion world was more of a pastime than a passion.

Once the film was over a short closing statement interview explained that 'Funny Girl' was Barbra Streisand's theatrical debut. On top of that she won an Academy Award for her performance in the film. It was at that moment I knew it was time for me to pursue my childhood dream of becoming an actress. I felt if Barbra could make it so could I. Carefully wiping my tears away, I lay down to rest, closed my eyes and dreamt of my future.

The next day as I went into work, Cassidy Lake, a dining room server, started flirting with me. He was six feet tall, slim, had dark brown hair, thick eyebrows, and was a bit of a comedian.

"Hey Lily, a bunch of us are going to the Four Winds tonight, want to come?"

The Four Winds was a dance club in the hotel that the staff went to almost every night.

"I have a boyfriend," I told him.

He asked me repeatedly. He even promised me that he wouldn't sit with me or bother me, he'd write me notes if he had anything to say. I laughed, gave in, and went with him. I fell hard for Cassidy, he was hilarious, the life of the party, everyone loved him! I soon found out his passion was playing. In the summer it was any water sport, like wind surfing, boating, water skiing, and in the winter, it was ice fishing, and downhill skiing. He was nothing but trouble, all he wanted to do was play with his friends, blow all his money, and party.

In September, Jamie came back from his tree planting job and he could tell something was wrong. I couldn't even get the words out of my mouth to break his heart. How do you tell the sweetest person you know that you don't love them anymore? When he asked me what was wrong, I started bawling.

He said, "You don't want to be with me anymore, do you?"

I told Jamie that I felt we'd drifted apart as people and that was it.

When I returned to Deerhurst later that day, Cassidy had left a note stating he'd taken off to Florida for a few months.

I felt sick to my stomach.

I had just ended a three-year relationship with a great guy, then the new one that begged me to give him a chance just takes off. I guess that meant I was single. I started partying with the other Deerhurst staff after work to pass the time.

When Cassidy returned from his three-month

holiday in Florida, we started dating, but he wasn't taking it seriously. I felt that I was more emotionally invested than he was and that didn't sit well with me. Then rumors started going around that he was fooling around with one or more of the other girls we worked with at the resort. I didn't want to believe it, so I chose not to.

Despite my denial, I had a feeling in the pit of my stomach that he was, in fact, cheating on me. I started ignoring him and gave him the cold shoulder whenever he'd come around. That's when things started to heat up. I don't play games, I wear my heart on my sleeve; therefore, guys always know where they stand with me. They also know when they are about to lose me.

In passing that night at work, Cassidy asked me if I was going to the club after work. I shrugged my shoulder and said, "No, why would I?" and kept walking. He had a lot of nerve asking me if I was going, without asking me to go with him.

Asshole.

Then he chased after me and said, "Lily. Babe, what's the matter?"

"What's the matter? Gee. I don't know. You beg me to go out with you, then take off for three months. When you return you act like a jackass and pretend I don't exist most of the time. On top of that there's a rumor going around that you're cheating on me with another girl. So, Cassidy, please tell me, are you fucking someone else?"

"No. I wouldn't do that. I love you Lily," he said.

It was the first time I ever heard him say that. I looked in his eyes, trying to gauge whether he was telling the truth. For all I knew, he'd said it to women all the time, maybe those words meant nothing to him.

So, I said the only thing that came to my mind. "Ok Cassidy. If you truly love me, prove it."

Cassidy looked a bit puzzled for a minute, not knowing what to say.

"Good-bye Cassidy," I said and took off walking down the empty hotel hallway.

"Wait! Lily. I don't want to lose you."

I continued walking, refusing to give Cassidy the benefit of the doubt.

"Why don't we move in together?"

I stopped dead in my tracks, turned around, and looked in those dark brown eyes.

"Are you serious?"

"Yes, of course I am. Why don't you move into my place? If that's what it takes to show you my love," he replied as he caught up to me.

This was the first time I ever sensed that Cassidy was serious. In my heart, I wanted our relationship to become better. It sure as hell was better than being single again so I agreed and one week later, we moved in together.

By this time, my parents decided to sell the store in Huntsville and move to Mississauga so they could be closer to their grandchildren. Even though I wasn't going with them, I felt glad that they finally decided to move back to the city and close to my sisters. If it wasn't for Cass, I would've gone with them.

Cassidy's place was a close drive from Deerhurst, which was convenient. Shortly after we moved in together, we were invited to one of the Vegas show dancer's weddings. It was a beautiful outdoor spring wedding, even though it snowed. Weddings always intensify love, and create a romantic ambience for me.

My sister, Layla, had to put a dress on a Greyhound bus for me so I had something nice to wear. There was no time to go to the city to shop. I made an appointment with a local hair stylist, she curled my hair, then weaved ribbon through my curls, which matched the lilac and cream colors that swirled through the dress.

At the reception that night, as Cassidy and I were

sharing a glass of champagne, he looked at me and said, "You look like a princess."

My heart melted, every woman should have a moment like that in her life. Beyond that experience, Cassidy quickly became a pain in the ass to live with. I had to constantly hassle him for his share of the bills. I paid for the car, the rent, the groceries. The relationship went from bad to worse. We frequently had fights that led to me packing up my car and threatening to move to the city to pursue my dream of becoming an actress, and to be close to my family again. I felt like I was his mother.

To say he was a slob was an understatement. He never did the dishes or laundry, emptied the trash, or cleaned around the house. Just before I almost lost it, Cassidy decided to give me an early birthday present, a trip for two to Aruba to help bring back the spark in our relationship. He'd put a small down payment on the trip but never came up with the rest of the money so instead of letting him lose that money, I paid the remaining balance.

Love can make you do stupid things. I think it even makes us temporarily insane sometimes.

We had two weeks and were on a budget. When we got to Aruba, all I wanted to do was spend the first few days on the beach and get some color before we started to explore the island. Instead, Cassidy argued with me every day to go on excursions such as snorkeling, scuba diving, or rent a Jeep to drive around the island. I eventually gave in just to shut him up.

Within the first three days, we did all those things and then we were out of money.

I thought this trip was supposed to make our relationship stronger but all we did was fight. He wouldn't listen to me about anything, including putting sunscreen on, so he got burnt to a pulp. When he started peeling, his forehead looked like alligator skin. He spent the rest of our vacation on the beach, wrapped in towels from head to toe, which made him even more annoying because he acted like a baby.

Every other day, one of us would pack up our suitcase and threaten to get on a plane and fly home early. Here I was, on an island I had no desire to be on, having a vacation from hell that was supposed to be my "birthday present" that I paid for. I wouldn't have picked Aruba if I was planning and paying for a trip.

Aruba was a volcanic island which meant that it was mostly desert because not much grows on volcanic rock. It was no tropical fantasy. I found the island dull, small, and boring. There was only one swimming pool in the whole hotel and it was the size of a blowup kiddie pool; holding no more than three people at a time.

I thought, the only saving grace had to be the beach, you can't fuck up Mother Nature.

Turns out, you can.

The water was so warm that it felt like I was swimming in a bathtub. There were no waves to play in. The water was completely calm the entire trip. I realize I'm sounding ungrateful, but this was a lot of money I had no intention on spending for a vacation I'd had no say in.

At one point, I was so bored that I fantasized about seeing a shark come out of the water onto the beach and swallow one of us up to end this nightmare.

I'm kidding.

Even the sharks found this place too boring.

The more time I spent with Cassidy, the more I realized he was a compulsive liar. When we got back from our trip, our next big fight was about the damage I found on my brand-new GMC Tracker. It looked like almost a hundred rocks had been shot at the rear end of my car. I discovered the damage when I was hand washing it in our driveway. I asked him what happened and he said that he had no idea. Then I overheard one of the guys at work say what an idiot Cassidy was for towing Greg's jeep with

Lily's car.

To get him to tell the truth, I had to threaten that I was going to call the car dealer, accuse them of selling me a damaged car and demand a new one.

Then, money from my bed side table would go missing. Money from my bank account went missing when I foolishly gave him my ATM card to do some deposits for me while I was getting my hair done at the mall. He withdrew the money in between the two transactions I asked him to do, then still tried to lie his way out of it and say it wasn't him. I thought I was to going to go crazy if I stayed with him.

I would scream and shout at the top of my lungs to try and get the truth out of him, but he only gave me lies upon lies.

We had great sex when we weren't fighting but if I did the math, that wasn't very often.

Back at Deerhurst, I had the day off and decided to wander around and enjoy the natural surroundings to help me become more at peace with Cassidy's constant bullshit. Near the lake, I saw Kim with a bunch of the girls from the ballroom. They invited me to join them for a ride on their friend's boat. It was a nice sized boat, seating at least six people. We stopped to take a dip in the water when we got too hot, then dried off in the sun over a few drinks.

The girls started a conversation about men and cheating, asking everyone, "If your boyfriend was cheating, would you want to know."

I said yes.

Suddenly, all the girl's eyes were on me. I felt like I was the only one not in on the joke; though, no one was laughing. Kim took me to the back of the boat and proceeded to tell me how Cassidy had been cheating on me with Barb all winter long. Barb was this pretty blond with a perfect body that was new to Deerhurst. I knew everyone but her, and I thought it was odd that no one had introduced us at the Christmas party. Barb worked in the same dining room section Cassidy worked. I knew I couldn't ignore this cheating scandal.

After three years of being together, that's what I got. I was humiliated. Three years of putting up with his bullshit. I should have broken up with him ages ago, despite fearing being single and alone.

Just then, my worst nightmare became true. The boat made a sharp turn toward the dining room gazebo. Low and behold, there they were, Cassidy and Barb, making out on the balcony. I got up from my seat, grabbed the boat's wheel, sped up, and headed straight to the shore.

As the boat got closer I slammed it into neutral, and blasted the boat's horn repeatedly. Cassidy was startled, and immediately broke his embrace with Barb. As he looked up toward the boat, I gave him the finger. The look on his face could only be described as shock and awe.

The girls began to laugh.

Maybe it was the alcohol in me, but the only thing that came to mind was yelling at the top of my lungs, "Hey fucko! I just found out I'm the only dumb ass in the company that didn't know you've been fucking Barb all winter! You're going wish you weren't born by the end of this summer, never mind the embarrassment you just experienced from getting caught in front of your boss and the whole dining room. I've been working with an entire company that knows you been fucking Barbie Doll behind my back for the past six months. Go fuck yourself because you won't be fucking me or her for the rest of the summer."

At first, I wasn't sure if he'd heard me, but judging by the hard slap Barb gave him before walking off and the expressions on the faces of the guests around him, I'm sure my message came across loud and clear.

Just then, all the girls on the boat gave me a cheer, while clinking their glasses with me. As I sat back down, trying to chill the fuck out, I could feel the adrenaline racing through my veins. As stressful as that was, I felt like a weight was suddenly lifted off my shoulders. There was no way Lily Monroe would put up with that shithead ever again. I didn't even care if my little scene ended up costing me my job. Sometimes in life you must stand up for yourself even if it means dealing with whatever consequences that may occur.

That night, during my shift, Eileen Twain was on stage singing her heart out. That night I felt as if God was trying to send me a message. The first song she sang was a cover song of Donna Summer's *No More Tears*.

Out of all the performers, everyone knew she would be a star. She had a natural beauty about her. The way her long, wavy, brown hair moved about as she swayed on stage, was striking. Her brown eyes were very still, often closing shut as she uttered every word through her rose-colored lips. This evening she wore a low cut, floor-length, stunningly green, sequined dress with a thigh high slit.

As I stood in the darkest corner of the room, she began to sing *Somewhere Out There*, written by James Horner. I was fighting back the tears. I didn't want anyone to see me. I still had customers to serve and a shift to finish. As the night ended and the customers started to leave, Twain sang one final number, *Over the Rainbow*, written by E.Y. Harburg. The way she sang that song brought tears to my eyes on any given night, but on this night, it drove my emotions over the edge. The tears started pouring down my cheeks. I knew I had to stop trying to find happiness with Cassidy and start working on finding what makes me happy. It was time to leave Deerhurst to pursue my dream of becoming an actress. I didn't want to end up like most people, bitter, and blame the world for my misery.

I had to find a way to make my dreams come true; my career dreams and my dreams of finding real and healthy love.

As the song ended, I could almost sense Twain looking at me from the stage. I know that she was going through her own life crisis at the time. Maybe that song moved her just as much as it did the people in the audience.

When the show was over and I was on my way out the door, Eileen happened to pass by me. We were wearing the exact same brown, leather jacket that I purchased only a few days before. She asked me how much I paid for it and I told her the amount. Although it was a strange coincidence, I felt deep down, we both wanted to say something more about what we were feeling but didn't have the nerve to express ourselves. Twain was quiet, she seemed shy and often kept to herself. Looking back now at this moment in my life, it's funny knowing that Eileen Twain became the world-famous, Shania Twain.

Deerhurst was called Hollywood North for a reason and although I hadn't become a star from working there, just being in the same vicinity as someone who did, inspired me to move on to pursue better things in my life.

I made my way home and broke up with Cassidy that very same night. Packed up all my things into my bright blue Tracker and drove off into the moonlight, never looking back.

Chapter Five
Star Struck

The year was nineteen ninety. I was twenty-four years old when I moved into my parent's place in Mississauga. I knew I had to be able to support myself so I fell back on the only job I knew how to pay the bills with, waitressing at a local Red Lobster.

I swore I would never give up on my passion of becoming a famous actor, despite still not having the adequate funds to attend a reputable acting school. One of my coworkers suggested I get some experience doing plays with one of the community theater groups in their area. If I felt my performance was worthy, he said I could invite agents to come see me and possibly get myself into the acting business that way. That sounded like a great idea to me so I instantly went and purchased a list of all the local theater groups at a local bookstore, specializing in drama.

After calling almost all the theater groups on the list, I finally managed to get my first real audition.

As I arrived inside the theater lobby, there were already several pretty girls around my age seated and armed with their latest black and white headshots and acting résumé. I was nervous as hell.

Unlike the competition, I had no acting training or experience whatsoever, only the sheer willpower to succeed. I knew nothing about the play and was going in blind. The only information I had was that I was reading for the character named Sissy. With a name like that, I certainly hoped I wasn't playing a wimp; although, at this point, I was willing to take on just about any role.

When my name was called, I stood up with my head held high and slowly entered the theater.

I nearly shit my pants.

I walked down the aisle toward the stage where two heads turned around staring right at me with blank expressions. The theater was massive, holding at least five hundred people. The room was dimly lit, minus the stage, which had a bright yellowish spot light on it. Once on stage, I stared out to the empty audience for what seemed like an eternity. All I could see were the plush red seats and a shadowy figure in the lighting booth. As my eyes began to focus, the director began to speak.

"Thank you for coming. My name is Alfie and this is the stage manager, Sophie."

I stood there like an idiot not knowing what to say or what the correct protocol was when doing an audition.

Finally, Alfie spoke again, "What is your name?" he said.

"Lily. Lily Monroe," I replied.

"What a beautiful name. Is that your real name or a stage name?" asked Alfie.

"My what?"

"Never mind. It doesn't matter. Please, tell me Lily, who are you reading for today?"

"Sissy," I answered.

As Alfie looked over at Sophie, she stood up and handed me the script. Trying to remain calm, I finally had the nerve to look Alfie in the face. He had a round friendly face, was balding with charcoal gray hair and a curly beard to match. His light green eyes reflected through the thin rimmed designer glasses that sat just slightly off center on his nose and seemed to suit him quite well. He wore a beige colored woolen sweater with black dress pants and polished black leather shoes, and spoke with a thick English accent. If I had to guess, he looked to be in his early fifties.

Sophie was just under four foot eight with a casual turquoise blue top and black dress pants. Her blond hair was neatly kept in pigtails. The more I observed her the more awkward she seemed, it was a feeling I could relate to. Sophie held a large purple notebook with several scribbles on the page, probably notes on each person's audition.

I did what was classically referred to as a cold reading, which is just a fancy term for reading an unrehearsed scene from the script. Sophie read for the other characters as Alfie surveyed my audition. My first read was terrible due to skipping a few of my lines and shaking all over. By the end of the audition, I just wanted to get the fuck out of there, but then, something magical happened.

"Are you nervous, Miss Monroe," Alfie asked.

"Well, kind of. You see, this is my first audition."

Alfie smiled, "Lily, before you read for me again, I want you to do something for me."

"Sure. What is it?"

"Stop fidgeting. Allow your body to be perfectly still. When you read the lines, I want you to do it much slower. Don't just read off the page, feel the emotions. Become Sissy. Pretend we are not in the room. Acting is believing you are another person. As Stanislavski always said, acting is reacting. It's about telling the audience the truth. Do you understand, Lily?"

"Yes, I think so," I replied.

"Good. Now, I want you to breathe in, breathe out, and when you are ready, start again."

I couldn't believe how nice Alfie was to me. I guess he wanted to see if I could take direction. He needed to figure out if he could work with me as an actor. It was the first time in my life someone offered me a chance and it meant the world to me. As I looked out into the empty audience, I took a deep breath and gave the audition of my life. The scene I read was for a stage version of the film, *Come Back to the Five and Dime, Jimmy Dean, Jimmy Dean* written by Ed Graczyk. One of the main characters, Mona, asks Sissy if she has ever dreamed what it would be like to have sex with someone famous and what it would be like to fall in love with them.

Back then, I had no idea how close to life this scene would become later in my life.

Long periods of loneliness can make you do crazy and stupid things. To those who've spent a lot of time alone, I imagine you may have a deeper understanding of exactly what one goes through. People dismiss loneliness like it's nothing or they themselves feel it's their fault. Like the character, Sissy, who was the wise one. Let me give you a piece of advice; there's no pill to fix it and nothing can make loneliness go away. It's unbearable sometimes.

After Cassidy and I broke up, I spent most of my free time alone. The days I would be off, I would sleep in if I could because I couldn't face spending another day by myself. No matter how much I cried or how much I begged for true love to enter my life, nothing seemed to change. Years went by, I eventually decided to take on the philosophy of living in the moment. At the time of this audition, I had no real boyfriend and all the previous men I've ever met, turned out to be wrong for me as a lifelong partner; yet, despite all of this, it made me a stronger person. Here I was, auditioning for a play with no experience only the conviction and certainty within myself that I knew I was meant for better things. I couldn't just sit there and watch my life pass me by, no one should.

It had already been four days since the audition and I hadn't heard back. I figured they chose someone else for the role and I moved on. As I got home from work, I saw my parents in the living room watching television.

"How was work?" asked my mother.

"Okay. Nothing special," I answered as I walked toward the kitchen.

"Who is Alfie?"

I stopped dead in my tracks and turned around.

"Alfie called? When? What did he say?"

My parents looked at each other with a very disappointed look on their face.

My mother answered, "He said you got the part."

A smile grew upon my face and turned upside down just as quickly when my mother glanced over at me with a real mean look in her eyes.

"Mom, what's the matter?"

"Since when did you decide to become an actress?"

I sat there in silence. I just couldn't believe her tone.

"When exactly where you going to tell us? I thought you wanted to pursue a career in the fashion business. I mean, why waste all your time and money on a college education just to throw it all away for a dream of being in show business, something that will never happen," yelled my mom.

I frowned, "I don't think I'm wasting my time."

My mother gave out a sinister laugh, "Lily, you've got to be kidding me! This is ridiculous! No one succeeds in show business. There are thousands of people trying to make it. What makes you so special? You're just going to end up a loser."

I could feel a fury of anger building up inside of me, like a volcano about to explode.

"Dad, what do you think about my decision? Let me guess, you'll just sit there in silence like you always do. It must be easy not having to make a decision or take a stance on anything," I said.

"Watch your manners, young lady," my mother yelled.

My father sighed, "Honey, we are just trying to make sure you don't make a mistake that you'll regret."

"Mistake? You think what I'm doing is a mistake! Let me tell you, I'm not a mistake. I am special and if you two can't see that; if your own closed mindedness can't allow you to let your own daughter try to make her dreams come true, then you seriously need to look in the mirror and ask yourselves what makes your lives so God damn special, instead of criticizing mine."

I stormed off to my room and slammed my bedroom door shut before crying myself to sleep.

When I woke up, the sadness was gone. I realized that Alfie giving me this chance had already taught me a valuable lesson. Even if I didn't have anyone's support, or a loved one to stand by me, if I believed in myself I could achieve anything.

Opening night had a sold-out audience.

At the end of the show, we received a standing ovation. I walked over to my dressing room, shut the door, took a deep breath, and looked at myself in the mirror. I reveled in the feeling of my accomplishment. While I removed my stage makeup, an enormous grin formed across my face. I was on a natural high. Who needs drugs or alcohol, all I needed to do was act. I kept replaying the best moments of the performance in my mind. It was all overwhelming; my head was spinning. My favorite moment was seeing the director sitting in the back row during my monologue. I could tell he was touched by my performance. For the first time in my life, I felt like every cell in my body was alive. Just then, I heard a soft knock on my dressing room door. Wanting this moment to last forever, I sluggishly got up and answered the door. To my surprise it was my parents. My father handed me a beautiful bouquet of fresh flowers then proceeded to tell me how much they enjoyed the show.

When I got home it was well after midnight. I hadn't eaten anything in over twelve hours so I crept into the kitchen and grabbed one of my father's beers and a slice of bread.

"You going to replace that beer?"

I jumped up, slamming the refrigerator door shut.

"Jesus Dad! You scared me," I breathed.

My father opened the fridge door, grabbing a bottle of beer, and sat down next to me at the kitchen table. I opened my beer and wolfed down the bread like I was starving to death.

"Lily, I want you to know your mother and I felt you did an incredible job tonight. In fact, we are willing to do anything to help you," said my father.

"What about that lecture you two gave me about pursuing a career…"

My father cut me off, "Forget it. That was in the past." He held his beer up high in a salutatory position. "To the best darn actress I know."

We clinked bottles and drank our beers in comfortable silence. In all my years of growing up this was the first time we ever had a private one-on-one conversation. I imagine this is what a father/son bonding moment must be like, if I were born a boy. I think for the most part, my Dad and I felt close without the need to talk. Looking back, I realize I inherited the stubbornness the rest of my family had. I'm proud of the strength that gave me to trust my instincts and follow my dreams. That grew into a strength with advantages, namely as I got older and went through some undesirable experiences, I developed a more aggressive, no bullshit attitude that vulnerable people need when they're faced with challenges in their lives. I may not have had many girlfriends growing up but at least I was slowly becoming my own woman and finding out what kind of person I truly was.

    A few months later, I was cast in the stage play, 'Nuts', based on the film with the same title. I played Claudia Draper, a high-class call girl who ends up killing a customer in self-defense and fights for the right to stand trial rather than be declared mentally incompetent. It gave me immense pleasure to know the role I was playing was originally done by Barbra Streisand in the film version. It was as if God was giving me a sign that I was on the right path, considering it was Barbra Streisand that provoked my passion and dream of becoming an actress in the first place. I kept auditioning for roles and landing a few here and there, mostly for stage productions. I was forging a path for myself with no training in acting or connections and realized that this couldn't go on forever, so with the guidance of a few cast members and directors I worked with; I signed up for some excellent acting courses.

    At twenty-six-years-old, I had at least a dozen

different character roles under my belt, that wasn't a lot, but at least I was on my way. I was still working at Red Lobster to have something to fall back on, when I finally got a call from my old pal, Alfie. He was opening a dinner theater and had already cast me in his first play without the need to audition and more importantly, I was getting paid. My first paid acting gig, I was ecstatic.

    I was warned about falling for my co-star Andy. He was 5'11", worked out a lot, was very fit, dark brown hair, grayish-blue eyes, a real smooth operator. He approached me gently with casual conversation at first. Then came the innocent invitations to hang out and have coffee after rehearsals to discuss how to make our performances better. I needed the escape. I didn't want to think about the years I wasted up north with Cassidy. Apparently, Andy was a dog though, and ended up with all his co-stars, but I didn't listen to the warnings. I started to hang out with him after rehearsals; he knew how to be romantic. When I wanted to hang out with him on Valentine's Day, after rehearsal, I knew I was in trouble, especially if the rumors were true. After dating for a week, I got a phone call from a strange number.

    It was Andy, calling from number I didn't recognize.

There was this invention called call display, not very many people had it at the time, and no one knew we had it, but we did.

After seeing him talking to a woman in her car after one of our shows, I had a feeling he was still seeing the girl he was calling his ex. I knew her name, then used my newfound investigation skills to get her phone number and address from my cousin. I started to become a detective, because I was starting to get tired of being played. My cousin and his so-called "Ex" were both fitness instructors for the rec centers in Mississauga. Everyone that taught classes had a list of everyone's name, number, and address, in case they needed a sub for a night off. I drove by her apartment building one night, and saw Andy's car parked in the parking lot. I fantasized about smashing his windows, then I decided to do something more useful with this information. I waited for the right moment to use the incriminating evidence I had gathered against him. I sat patiently, waiting for the day her phone number popped up on my call display. I made sure I didn't answer. I waited and called back, asking who called me from there. Knowing damn well it was him.

See, she knew who I was too, because she had come to see our play. As soon as she asked who was calling, and

I told her my name, she knew who I was.

She said, "I'll tell Andy you called."

I said, "Don't bother, I don't ever want to speak to him again."

She asked me why, then we had a little chit chat, I told her the truth. She replied by saying she was getting old, she was thirty-three, she wanted children, and was afraid of being alone. She said she was probably going to stay with him. I told her that was her business and to watch her wallet.

I was certain he had stolen money from me when we were on a romantic getaway in Niagara. She stated that she thought he'd stolen from her too, but didn't want to believe it.

At least now she knew it was true. If she wanted to live in denial, that was her choice. I wished her luck and said goodbye. People will not walk away from a bad relationship; at least not until they're ready, it doesn't matter what you tell them.

I had done my part by letting her know exactly whom she was dealing with. The ball was in her court. At least now she could make an informed choice, let him stay knowing he was playing her or kick him out knowing she wasn't losing anyone special.

Of course, by letting him stay, she was making a conscience decision to let someone take advantage of her. This is what victims eventually need to own up to and accept. At some point, if we are lucky enough to find out we are being used, and we stay in that relationship, we become the one responsible for our unhappiness and pain. He was living with her for free and stealing from her. Her suspicions had now been confirmed. How could she not be sure what she was going to do? I know how, that damn crippling disease called loneliness.

However, ignoring the warning signs, the red flags is not a wise choice. I fall hard and fast, I understand the feeling of being head over heels for someone you just met. I'm not saying it's easy, but I'm telling you, getting away from a bad person early on is less damaging than what you're going to go through years later. My love life was starting to feel like a baseball game. Andy had struck out, it was batter up, who and what was the universe going to bring me next.

We had a friendly close-knit staff at Red Lobster. I was single for the first time since I'd returned to the city. A group of us started hanging out together. We went clubbing, had house parties, pool parties, went on road trips to the States together.

Ian was one of the group members and one of my coworkers that truly cared about me. He was very muscular, and tall, standing at 5'10", black, very good looking, nice family, lived with his parents in a big house. He was putting himself through university by serving at Red Lobster, and was obsessed with working out. He even made his girlfriend get in kick ass shape.

Ian had his shit together, if only we were meant to be with each other. He drove me home from work one afternoon and gave me a firm lecture on how naïve I was. He took it upon himself to educate me on the male breed, called "The Player". Men that had several women, who all thought they were his one and only. One would leave out the front door, just as the other arrived in the back. Women that gave them money for rent, clothes, car payments, and these guys didn't work.

I'm not sure I would've even believed him if I hadn't just experienced it with my own eyes. This was a whole new disgusting level of deceit than what I'd experienced up north. How do these guys look at themselves in the mirror? I don't know how any man can respect himself, when he just uses women for money. What kind of world was I living in? How was I going to meet a great guy if this was the definition of dating in the city?

I would lie in bed, praying to God night after night, with tears in my eyes, asking him to bring me the love of my life, a true love, or at least a best friend.

CHAPTER SIX
Night Out

Then God gave me Betsy. She was a bright, funny, charismatic, energetic coworker, who suddenly became my new best friend! We spent all our free time together. We were inseparable.

She only listened to hip-hop, reggae, and R&B, which meant we only went to clubs that played that music. Which also meant, for the first time in my life, only being exposed to black men. That was most of the crowd that hung out at these clubs.

That's who I started dating. When it became the only type of man I dated, my parents got annoyed. They didn't understand why it had to be exclusively black men, why couldn't I throw a white guy into the mix. I didn't have the answer, nor did I care to analyze or discuss it, it just simply was.

It was a Friday night in the summer, Betsy and I were in line to get into the club, *Government,* she was complaining that it was too hot and she wanted to leave. She was nineteen, and had the hot flashes of a woman going through menopause. I was meeting up with a hot bouncer that hit on me the week before and was determined to stay. I kept ignoring her complaints and hoped she would stop. There was no sense discussing anything with her, she was hot tempered and irrational.

I finally got close enough to the doorman to tell him we were on Tony's list. He immediately waved us in. We made our way through the crowded club and went straight to the bar, grabbed a drink, and then straight to the dance floor. We were dancing, laughing, then suddenly, I see this guy staring at me from a distance. I discreetly leaned into my friend to whisper in her ear to check him out, but he was clever, he caught on, and bolted. A short while later, he approached me outside on the patio, his name was Arthur.

I laughed., he didn't look like an Arthur. He was Jamaican, a little muscular, under six feet tall.

Next thing I know, we're kissing. Alcohol's an aphrodisiac for me. If I drink, someone's getting kissed, and hopefully it's someone hot.

Arthur and I were having this amazing first kiss. Fireworks were going off, in my head of course. This isn't "The Bachelorette". Suddenly, someone's pulling on my belt and yanking me away from him.

I look up to see who? Betsy.

I give her a "what the fuck?" look and folded my arms, waiting for her to tell me why she'd just ruined that fantastic moment.

That was one of the best kisses I've ever had.

She tells me that the guy I was supposed to meet up with showed up, came outside, and saw me making out with someone else.

Oops, uh oh, now what? I guess I should go try to find him and apologize. I walked away from Arthur and went inside. I found the other guy leaning against the bar with a bottle of beer in his hand. He was pissed and as soon as his eyes landed on me, he slammed it down on the counter, before storming out of the club. I was mad that he didn't even give me the chance to explain or even talk to him, but then again, there really is no legitimate excuse. I just shouldn't have put myself in that position to begin with. The night was ruined and I had no desire to be in this atmosphere anymore, so Betsy and I decided to leave after she'd given her number to one of Arthur's friends.

Fast forward to the next week, Betsy is supposed to meet the guy she gave her number to at the club, and I'm supposed to meet that guy that caught me kissing Arthur.

Of course, Arthur shows up at the club with Betsy's date.

I'm thinking, *Are you for real?*

I'm still in shit from last week, the last thing I need is a replay.

I kept looking around to see if my date had showed up or not. I'm outside the club and Arthur is standing next to me. He cracks a joke about me looking nervous, saying, with a laugh, "What's up? Is that guy supposed to be here?"

I'm thinking, *Yes, dumb ass! He is and I don't need you around when he does.*

But, I don't say that. I just let out a nervous giggle.

He puts his arm around my shoulder and walks me into the club. I still didn't know what to think of him. I was too busy to worry about these two men. My time was spent working, spending time with Betsy, doing plays, and working out. I was never home. I wasn't thinking about dating anyone. And sure enough, after two years of being single, the second I'm too busy to care is when two guys decide to start pursuing me. Since neither of them could get a hold of me at home, Tony, the hot bouncer, comes looking for me at work. I wasn't there at the time.

Arthur starts calling me at work, which every waitress knows is a big NO. Finally, the hostess got pissed and put him on hold, then came and told me I had to get on the phone and tell him to stop calling. That's how Arthur finally got a hold of me and got the chance to talk me into going on a date with him.

Arthur was funny, confident, and affectionate and before I knew it, I was sleeping over at his place every night.

We got serious, fast, I fell for him. We had good chemistry, and I loved that he wanted me around all the time. He even said he'd met me just in time. I'm not sure what he meant by that at the time, but I think the answer was meant to come to me, down the road. What I did know is that this was exactly what I wanted in my life, a real relationship. It had been a couple of years since I was with Cassidy, that's the longest I'd ever been single. When I thought about it, I decided that was two years too long.

Arthur lived with his half-brother in a ground level apartment in Toronto. His brother's girlfriend would stay over every weekend and every Sunday morning she would come in our room, jump in bed with us to wake us up, say good morning, and chat. We were one big happy family.

Betsy started getting mad that I wasn't spending any time with her, but all she wanted to do was go clubbing. I didn't feel like dealing with the bitchy attitude she was giving me, so I ignored her calls. I wasn't interested in constantly being pressured by her to go clubbing. I wasn't a huge fan of that scene when I was single, I certainly didn't want to go when I had a boyfriend.

It's annoying being hit on by guys who refuse to leave you alone even after you tell them you have a boyfriend. I don't consider it a good time to be out arguing with guys that are trying to get laid. I was a girlfriend/boyfriend type of girl, not a party girl.

Arthur also gave me an ultimatum between clubbing with Betsy or a relationship with him. I chose him and Betsy and I never talked again.

It had been a few months; everything was going great between us. Until, the night I was at his place alone while he was having his weekly *Dungeons and Dragons* night with the boys. He didn't have a car, so I was supposed to pick him up, when his phone rang, I answered it, thinking it was him telling me he was ready. To be honest, part of it was to see who was the cause of the ridiculous amount of missed calls that showed up on his call display. Guys do not call each other that much, there had to be girls calling him.

I was right, it was a girl, a girl who had hung out with Arthur and his friends the weekend before. Nothing had happened she said, but he was flirting with her, and they were keeping in touch. I felt shaky and sick to my stomach. As soon as I hung up, he called, asking where I was. I said that I was on my way. He seemed mad, it was like he knew I just answered that call from that girl.

When we get back to his place, he stomped inside and started yelling at me. He knew something was wrong, he sensed it in my voice the second I answered the phone, and he was trying to turn his deceitful behavior around on me.

I grabbed my stuff, said we're through, and headed toward the door. He pushed me from behind. I told him not to ever touch me like that again, or he'd be sorry, then I left.

He chased me out the door and asked me to come back. I kept on walking, got in my car, and drove home. He called me the second I walked in the door and asked me to come back.

I did. It was the weakest thing that I'd ever done in my life. I can't say things were ever the same or that I fully trusted him, but I did love him and I believed in our love.

Shortly after that night, Arthur had a fire in his

place. He lost everything. I tried to replace as much of it as I could, during Christmas that year. Because his family was in Jamaica, he had to move into the basement of a close friend of his.

The basement he moved into, came with three screaming kids that lived above us. Every morning at six, these kids would have a screaming fucking fit about getting up, dressed, and fed to go to school. It was brutal. He didn't want me to sleep at my house and I couldn't sleep at his. It had been months of no sleep and I was at the end of my rope. I was exhausted, burnt out, and my nerves were shot. I was losing it.

It was my turn to give Arthur an ultimatum, move out or I'm out. He started looking for a new two-bedroom place with one of his friends. They settled for the basement of a triplex. It was infested with cockroaches.

I could've been living in my parents' perfectly clean condo. I am a fool for love.

While I was in Ryerson Theatre School, studying my ass off, and Arthur was the head manager of a retail store, I started to have that sick feeling in my stomach that I get when my boyfriends are cheating on me. I couldn't even touch him when I lied next to him in bed at night. I knew my suspicions that he was sneaking around behind my back were probably true.

He would go clubbing every weekend without me. I hated it, we fought every day about it. It didn't stop him; the entire three years we were together, he never missed one Saturday night at the clubs; yet, I wasn't allowed to go to any clubs without him. He was probably terrified I'd run into him with one of his other women.

We broke up a few times, I'd pack my car, then unpack my car. I could make it out the door, but not up those steps. Arthur would see that my car was still parked out back, open the door, reach out his hand and pull me back in. We would hug and the intensity from his embrace convinced me that he truly loved me. After three years of this, I was getting tired of being played. It was time to reinstate my detective skills. Arthur went out of town for business, I wasn't living with him at the time, we were on a break. I snuck into his apartment while he was away. Let's call it an extraction mission to recover lost items that belonged to me. Upon entering the apartment and seeing paperwork that was in plain sight, it became a recon mission.

If he was cheating, I wanted solid proof. It was impossible to see any of his paperwork when I lived there, he would instantly rip up any bill and throw it out. As soon as I walked through the front door there it was on the kitchen counter, the holy grail, his phone bill. It proved to be a very valuable document. I started to examine all the calls listed, then I focused only on the numbers he called late at night, then I narrowed it down to the duration of those late-night phone calls. Those were the numbers I recorded, I thought they'd be a good start. It certainly wasn't his buddy he was pouring his heart out to at 3 A.M. for over an hour. Next was the bedroom, what goodies was I going to find there? Right on the computer desk was a tiny yellow Post-it with numerous four digit codes written on it. I had never seen that before, that must be important. It turns out it was. On that tiny piece of paper were the codes to his cell phone voice mail and his computer. Both of which contained a wealth of information the second I hacked into them. First was the cell phone, which contained numerous saved voice mails from other girls, next was the key I found that unlocked this box he had kept under the bed the entire time we were together, which was full of love letters from other women, and finally were the numbers I called that led to girls he was fooling around with.

  I'm proud of the detective work I did, even though it didn't make me leave him for good at that moment, it led to the finale. I don't care if people think it's wrong and disgusting. It is disgusting to lie and cheat, and play with someone's heart. I needed to know beyond a reasonable doubt that the man I was in love with was cheating. Or I would never have the courage to leave him. Those are the only conditions I could walk away on, with no regret, and never look back.

He was never going to admit it. I had caught him on top of another woman and he still tried to lie his way out of it, by saying, "I didn't cheat. I wasn't inside her!"

My friends from Ryerson would try and talk some sense into me. They said, "Wow, that one day a month when he's nice and treats you good must be one hell of an amazing day to keep you there, putting up with all his bullshit."

They were kind about it. They never pushed me to leave him. They only offered me advice a couple of times over the years. Other than that, they left the topic alone.

When Arthur and I had a good day, it was the best. He brought out the best in me, a funny, wacky side that I didn't even know existed before I met him. We had a playful, intelligent, creative, and entertaining relationship. When we were goofing around and having fun, his friends would say we were perfect for each other.

We both had quiet sides that matched perfectly as well. We would go for long walks on warm summer nights, he would put his hand in my back pocket, and neither of us needed to say a word. On warm summer days, we would go sit by Lake Ontario. I would put my head on his lap, stare at the water, and dream of our future together. I love looking out at water. Pools, oceans, lakes, I could stare at them for days.

He would tell me stories to help me sleep at night when I was worried or upset. We were both into working out and staying in shape; although, I was never thin enough for him. Which would probably give most girls an eating disorder, but not me. I just resorted to eating candy bars in my car before I went inside the apartment, which come to think of it, kind of is a disorder.

The same person that could bring out the best in me, could bring out the worst. He was always criticizing me, trying to convince me that I wasn't a nice person. He would constantly tell me I was too overweight to play the roles I wanted to play. He made several attempts to make me feel worthless. There were times he came close.

Staying with him would eventually destroy my self-esteem until I had no confidence, then I'd probably never leave. I wasn't going to let my life be like that, I had to demand better for myself. I made myself a promise that unhealthy, abusive people would be cast out of my life instantly, from here on in.

I didn't have the time to catch him while I was putting myself through university. He would always wait until I was studying for an exam at my girlfriend's place before he would disappear. I wasn't going to sacrifice my exam grade, when he didn't answer either phone, to chase him around the city. I had no idea where to start. I didn't think for one second he'd be fucking someone in our own bed.

The second I was done with university was a whole different story. Once I finished school, I had all the time in the world to go chasing him. The first time he didn't answer the phone at one in the morning, after I told him I was going to sleep at my parent's place, I hopped in my car and drove to straight to our place. There it was, the undeniable, visual proof I thought I needed to get away from him for good. I walked inside, went straight to the bedroom, and there he was, lying naked on top of another girl. I don't know if they were doing it or not, but I gladly interrupted whatever was going on. I waited in the living room for him to get dressed. We fought, he looked scary. When I asked him to give me back the watch I had given him as a gift, which was my sister's bright idea, it pushed him over the edge. He grabbed the watch, ripped it off his wrist, and threw it at me. I thought he was going to hit me.

I refused to leave until he made her leave. He wouldn't make her leave. My body temperature was dropping from the stress; I was so cold I was shaking.

After shaking for two hours, I'd had enough. He wasn't going to give in and make her leave, I decided it was time to go. I asked him to step away from the door. I wasn't going to walk past him, he looked terrifying. I think he wanted to kill me. He wouldn't move an inch, and I couldn't get past him without brushing his shoulder, he was guarding the only exit. I didn't want to get sick over this bullshit, I got up and moved toward the door to leave. Before I even reached the door knob, he grabbed me, threw me on the couch, and started choking me. I was right, he did want to kill me. Go figure. He was the cheater; yet, he was the one infuriated. Mad at me because I caught him? Fucking crazy human beings in this world we live in. I tried to scream out. The stupid girl in the bedroom didn't even come out to rescue me.

Just before I was about to pass out, he let go. That's when I made my move. I instantly jumped up off the couch, grabbed my purse, and ran out the door. I can't believe I was in that situation. I was not brought up to be a victim. I always thought I'd kick a guy's ass if he dared to put a finger on me. Of course, it's always easy to say I'd never put up with that, that would never happen to me, I would never be in that situation, until you're in that situation. I came to realize it was not wise for me to judge others as there were many situations that I ended up being in myself. I learned to never say never.

I had a good childhood. I thought for sure I'd have a bright future, a good job, a wonderful husband. You can head down the right path, educate yourself, work hard, I don't care what anyone says, for some of us, that doesn't equal success. I was lost as to how to gain control of my life and turn things around. No one knows what obstacles we might have to overcome, and how to deal with those obstacles. I did things I wish I never did; I was beginning to comprehend the desperate acts that come from being at our lowest.

I've been judged for the way I lived during the years I was single, by people who didn't even make the slightest attempt to understand why. People are incapable of understanding what they haven't been through. That's why I work hard at reminding myself not to undermine other people's struggles.

My relationship with Arthur reminds me of the Lauryn Hill song, *Ex-Factor*.

No one hurt me more than you, and no one ever will…

Chapter Seven
Changes

    My Dad wanted me to press charges, I said no, I wasn't going to ruin his life. He had a promising future, he was a hard worker, and moving up fast in his company. Luckily, my long hair hid the marks on my neck. I went into work the next day feeling shaky, but acted as if nothing had happened. After the lunch rush was over, I found myself staring blankly at the overcast sky through the glass windows of Red Lobster. What am I doing here? Is this what life's about? Why do I always seem to attract cheaters? How can I fill this empty void deep inside me? I need a purpose in life. Out of the corner of my eye I noticed Eileen staring at me.

    "Lily. Are you okay?" she asked.

    "Huh? Oh, sure, I'm fine." I half lied.

    Eileen shook her head, "Honey, you don't look fine.

I called your name over five times."

"Really? Look, I'm sorry, it's just, well, I broke up with Arthur last night," I said.

Eileen gave me a hug and smiled. It was strange coming from her since we barely knew each other.

"So, what did he do this time?"

"I caught him in bed with another woman," I admitted.

She gasped, "No. You didn't."

I nodded my head.

"I just don't get it. I'm an attractive woman with a great personality; yet, I always seem to attract cheaters. God! Why am I telling you all this?"

She reassuringly placed her hand on my shoulder, "It's okay, Lily. I understand."

"Thanks Eileen, I really appreciate you listening. You know, we should hang out more often."

"Can't. I'm moving out to B.C."

"When?" I asked.

"In five days to be exact. That's why I came over to you so I could say goodbye. Today's my last day."

"I'm coming with you." I said.

She laughed, "Are you crazy?"

"Yep, just a little bit. What I need is a change of

scenery, a chance to start over again. We'll drive to B.C. through the northern part of the U.S."

"What are you going to do for a job?" she asked.

"I've heard Vancouver is busy with film and television work. I just graduated from Ryerson Theatre School, who knows? Maybe that's where I was meant to go to make a name for myself in the acting world. Come on, what do you say?"

Eileen paused for a moment, "Okay. sounds like fun to me."

Without giving it a second thought, I immediately quit Red Lobster. Sometimes in life you should just go for the opportunity in front of you. I walked outside to my car and got in. As I turned the key, there was dead silence. No way, come on, this can't be happening. The engine wouldn't start. It was as if some force was trying to keep me there. I tried the key again and again, producing the same results. As I sat there ready to have a complete nervous breakdown, all I could see was the navy blue Red Lobster sign staring back at me as if it was mocking me. There was no way I was going to go back in there to ask for help. All my moves had to be forward, there was no turning back. My boss told me I should just take a leave of absence instead of quitting, that way if things don't work out I can have my job back, which means he doesn't think I'm going to make it. I can't go back in there and ask them to call a tow truck, I had to figure this out on my own.

Even though this Red Lobster was in a small plaza there was not a payphone in sight. It was a windy October afternoon, I shivered from the winter chill that was in the air as I got out of my car. I noticed the autumn leaves on the ground and took this as a literal sign that I was turning over a new leaf and decided to wander off until I found the help I so desperately needed.

Five and a half blocks later, I stumbled upon a gas station with a working payphone. I searched frantically through the yellow pages until I found the listing for all the local tow trucks in the area. A company called 24/7 Towing caught my eye. Obviously, they would be available with a name like that.

I tried to clean the phone as much as I could with my sleeve, then dialed the number. "Twenty-Four Seven, what is your location?" asked the man on the other end.

I gave the address, hung up the phone, wiped my ear, and walked back to my car.

As I sat in my car to keep warm, I noticed the monstrous tow truck approaching in my rearview mirror. The truck was white and olive green. I got out of my car and flagged it down. As the tow truck came to a stop the driver got out and slammed the door shut. He seemed pissed. I was the one with the broken car, I don't know what his problem was. He was in his forties about six feet tall with a massive beer belly. Probably hasn't been laid in a while, how was that my fault? A half-smoked cigarette dangled between his chapped lips and scruffy beard. On the left side of his blue shirt was a patch with the company logo while the name James was hand-stitched on the right in bright red.

    James walked over to my car and greeted me with a friendly gesture of spitting on the ground.

    Nice.

    "Is this her?"

    I'm certain he would've called it a him if it was a sports car. I stood there staring at him. Praying to God he wasn't going to rip me off.

    "Look lady, I don't have all day, so how bout you answer me?"

    "Yes, that's my car," I said.

    "You got a mechanic? Where do you want it to be towed to?"

    I groaned, "I don't know what to do. It was working fine this morning, now the engine won't start, this hasn't happened before."

"You want to junk it or repair it," asked James.

"Repair it obviously, I'm not rich and it's not a piece of junk, is it?"

"Lady, it ain't my place to say. I could take you to a mechanic, might be a good place to start," he snorted.

"Well, the thing is, I don't know any mechanics. I was kind of hoping you might know someone I could trust."

James gave out a large sigh, shrugged his shoulders, and told me to get in the truck. As I watched him attach my car to the back of the tow, I noticed some of the servers at the Red Lobster were looking out the window at us. I was so embarrassed. I quit my job, take a huge risk and say I'm moving out west and I can't even make it out of the parking lot. No grand exit happening here. I hope this wasn't a sign of what lay ahead of me.

Once everything was safely secured James hopped in the truck and we drove away.

*** ***

The tow truck stopped in front of *Joe's Auto Repair*. "This is it. Wait here," said James.

I looked at the time on the truck stereo. These two

seemed shady, it was two in the afternoon. If it wasn't for the daylight I would have left, then and there. As my paranoia started to build, I quickly flipped my head around as my ears picked up the sound of metal clanking in the wind. The garage door began to rise, revealing James and a much shorter man in his mid-fifties with silver hair, wearing mechanics overalls covered in grease. I locked the door and rolled down my window ever so slightly as the two of them approached me.

"Joe, this is the lady I was telling you about."

Joe nodded toward me, "Hi Miss, James told me you need a mechanic."

"Yes. I just want to know if it's worth repairing," I said.

"Sure thing, but it's going to cost you."

"How much?"

"Depends on what needs fixin'. If your car is a lemon, we'll scrap it for you, junkyard might give you a hundred for it, if you're lucky," Joe replied.

"How can I trust you?"

Joe gave James a sour look.

"Excuse me Miss, but I think my friend and I are doing you a favor. If you don't like my offer I'm sure James can drop you off someplace else.

I sighed, "Sorry. I'm a little stressed out. I just quit my job, broke up with my boyfriend, and decided to move out west all in the last twenty-four hours, and then my car broke down."

"No harm done. Why don't you sit down in my office and have a cup of coffee? That way you can watch me work on your car so you don't think I'm trying to rip you off. How's that sound?" Joe asked.

"That would be great, thanks."

Joe's office was small and narrow. A tall aluminum percolator sat neatly to my left on a worn out, square shaped, mahogany table. Beside it laid a stack of Styrofoam cups and a half-liter carton of milk. Pens and pencils, with oil stains on them, rested in a large gray coffee mug. The walls were covered with black picture frames containing various certificates, mechanic licenses and photos of old-fashioned cars. Several dingy filing cabinets ran flush against the walls beside the water cooler. The door to Joe's office was quite sturdy and made entirely of wood, minus the glass window in the center of the frame. I walked over to the percolator and poured myself a coffee against my better judgment. The place was filthy, but desperate times called for desperate measures, and coffee always made things better. The milk felt cold as I gently poured it into my cup. The coffee tasted better than I thought it would.

I looked up as Joe came through the door with a big grin on his face.

"Any luck?"

"Oh yes. You better believe it. Follow me, I want to show you something," Joe opened the hood, "Has this vehicle ever been in an accident?"

"No. My ex-boyfriend towed his buddy's jeep out of the mud with it, but that's it."

"Hmmm. That's strange, see these parts here?"

I peered inside the hood, pretending I knew what the hell he was talking about.

"Those parts have tiny holes in them; my guess is from rock damage. When's the last time you had your car looked at?"

"There were dents on the paint from the tow, I didn't know the rocks hit inside. Fuckin' Cassidy. I'd like to strangle him right now. I'd never had mechanical problems. I never had a reason to service it. I grew up in a small town and I just kind of looked after the car myself."

Joe chuckled, "That explains it. You really should get your car looked at once, if not twice, a year."

"Joe, I don't mean to be abrupt, but cut to the chase, can you repair it or not?"

Joe glanced at me with a very serious look before saying, "Sorry to say this, but the overall cost to repair it is more than the vehicle is worth. There have been years of compound damage in the engine, muffler, fuel tank…"

I put my hands up to stop them, "Okay, okay. I get the picture."

"Lady…" James started.

"My name is not lady, it's Lily."

"Lily," he paused, "Tell you what. I'll give you three hundred bucks, cash, and a hundred to Joe."

I frowned, "Joe just said it was worth five hundred."

"Yes, but I'm also running a business. You can take a chance and try to get it fixed somewhere else and pay even more money for them to tell you the same thing. It's up to you, take it or leave it."

I carefully focused on both, James and Joe. Was this some sort of scam that they pulled on innocent bystanders or was my car done for? As much as I didn't want to admit it, my gut instincts told me they were telling the truth. After all, my car was ten years old, maybe that was it for old Bessy.

I tossed James my car keys and took the money.

"James? I was wondering if you could give me a

ride home? I don't want to spend money on a cab, not after a day like today. Please?"

James gave out another sigh, "I guess, but it better be close or you can forget it."

We got in the tow truck and pulled out of the parking lot.

"Where to?"

I turned my face away from James and began crying.

"What's wrong now?" he asked.

"Nothing in my life seems right. My boyfriend cheated on me. I have no career, no job. I owe Ryerson money, and now my car broke down."

"Can't you just by a new one?"

I groaned, "You don't understand. My friend and I are supposed to be leaving in five days to B.C."

"Why don't the two of you fly instead? It would save a lot of time," James said as he pressed the gas and made his way through the traffic light.

"I thought about that, but I was really looking forward to our road trip and having a car out there. I have three years of stress to detox from and a long drive would be perfect for my soul right now. It's complicated."

He looked over at me in mock disgust. "Is this some

sort of girly thing?"

I laughed as I wiped the tears from my face.

"It sounds to me like you need a new car, maybe that will give you a new outlook on life."

"That's exactly what I need. The problem is, I'm unemployed, who's going to sell me a car?"

"Lily, you're talking to the right person. Now let me think. What would be the perfect car for someone in your situation, someone starting over, and driving across the country?" he pondered his question for a moment before saying, "I got it!"

"You do? What is it? How much is it? Where is it? What's it look like?"

"You want to see it now?"

I lit up in excitement, "Yes, of course, if we can, that would be great!"

"Okay. Next stop, the car of your life."

The tow truck pulled up to a metallic silver building, shaped like a trapezoid, encased by floor-to-ceiling glass windows. It was nearly four thirty, the sun was beginning to set, casting a bright yellow tinge that reflected on the windows. Finally, a positive sign. It looked like the heavens were shining down on this showroom.

I looked up toward the sky and saw four shiny

chrome rings attached together. I knew that was the symbol for the type of car only rich people bought.

"Are you sure this is the right spot?" I asked.

"Yep. This is it."

He took out a pen and his business card, flipped it on its back and proceeded to write something down.

"Here. Take this and show it to the dealer. He'll know what to do," said James.

"Thanks, I really appreciate your help," I said.

"You take care."

I took his card, shook his hand, and walked into the dealership. I noticed a small sign hanging above the double doors that read *Audi*.

A middle-aged man, wearing a navy suit and a striped colored tie, approached me.

"Can I help you, Miss?"

"I'm not sure. A colleague of mine suggested you might be the right place to consider purchasing a new vehicle," I said.

"Certainly. My name is Tony. Is there a specific type of car you are looking for?"

"I don't know. A car that works I guess?"

Tony nodded his head in agreement accompanied with one of the most intense plastic smiles I've ever seen.

"Fair enough. What exactly is it that you plan on doing with this car? Are you planning on driving to work, short distances, long distances?"

I stopped him, "Long distances. I'm going to be driving from Toronto to Vancouver."

I reached inside my purse and handed over the business card, "Here, maybe this will help."

His smile faltered as he looked down at the card. He took it, read it, then looked back up at me with that same plastic smile, "Follow me. You're in for a real treat."

Tony walked me over to a silver *Audi,* two-door convertible.

"This is the nineteen ninety-five *Audi* Cabriolet. Comes with a V6, two point eight-liter engine, and can reach sixty miles per hour in nine point six seconds. Go on, have a seat," he opened the door and instructed me to get in. I did and I immediately felt like I belonged.

Beside the clutch lay three gauges measuring battery, oil pressure and temperature. The two-toned all leather seats in black and gray oozed sexiness.

"Would you like to give it a spin?" asked Tony.

Within moments, I was behind the wheel in their back lot. The feel of the car was incredible. I didn't have to be a car expert to know this was luxury. I pulled the car to a complete stop.

"How much is it?"

"Thirty-six thousand dollars," said Tony.

"That's ridiculous, I can't afford that, can you go any lower?"

"Thirty-five thousand dollars, but that's as low as I go," he replied.

I sighed, "I don't have that kind of money."

"Tell you what. You put five thousand down and pay the rest in monthly installments," said Tony.

"I don't know. Maybe this is a bad idea," I said.

"Miss, let me give you a piece of advice. Life is too short. I see millions of people every day that are miserable. This is the perfect car for you, if you don't buy it, I can easily sell it for that price, sorry that's the best I can do. Take a minute, think about it."

I handed Tony my credit card, closed my eyes and hoped it would go through. Hopefully I didn't just make the biggest mistake of my life.

Chapter Eight
Moving Out West

Five days later, I'm packing the trunk of my new car with my duvet, two suitcases full of clothes, and shoes, trying to make sure there is enough space for Eileen and her stuff. Lucky for me most of her belongings were being shipped to her parents' house in Vancouver.

Both my parents started crying.

I hugged them goodbye and drove off. It was gut wrenchingly hard to drive away from my parents as tears poured down their cheeks, but, at this point in time, moving away seemed like the best thing to do. I had multiples urges to turn around and drive home, but instead, I sucked up my own tears, fears, doubts, sadness, found an inner strength I had no idea I had, and kept on driving.

When I arrived, Eileen was already on the sidewalk, dressed in her winter jacket, with suitcase in hand.

"Since when do you drive a car like this?" asked Eileen.

I half smiled, "Don't even ask, I bought it a few days ago. Figured we might as well drive in style."

"You're the boss."

Eileen squeezed her bag into the trunk and got in the passenger's side. Taking one last swig of my large vanilla latte, I zipped up my winter jacket, put on my leather racing gloves, and started the ignition.

"Buckle up. Next stop, Vancouver B.C. "

I put the car into first gear and we sped onto the highway. Not caring that it was chilly, I pushed a button and the roof opened.

"Whoo-hoo!"
"Lily, you're crazy. It's the middle of October."

I looked over at Eileen and smiled. We both burst out laughing. I could tell Eileen was going to be easy to get along with and was glad she was the one I was on this road trip with. The cold wind blowing across my face felt exhilarating. I put the car in overdrive, going over one hundred miles per hour. Besides the adrenaline rush, I had a more practical reason for speeding. The cost of the car depleted most of the funds left in my bank account. I had to get us to Vancouver quick and find work immediately no matter what the cost.

One day and five hours later, we hit the badlands in Western South Dakota. Having not slept in over twenty-four hours, Eileen and I decided to stop the car and stretch our legs. Numerous clay colored, sedimentary rock formations of varied shapes and sizes seemed to go on for thousands of miles. As I wandered across the grasslands, I felt a great sadness fill my heart because these surroundings reminded me so much of myself and where I was in my life. Although I'm sure wildlife existed in such a barren place, to me all I could see was complete emptiness, representing pages of time. A scenic wonderland filled with nothing but old fossils. Was this trip a mistake on my part or am I meant to learn something from this experience?

"Lily, what's the matter," asked Eileen.

"Hmm? Oh, it's nothing."

"You're not a very good liar. Come on, you can tell me."

I stood there in silence, not wanting to bring her down to my level. I owed her that much.

"I know just the thing to cheer you up," Eileen lay down on the ground like a snow angel.

"What are you doing?"

She patted the spot next to her and smiled up at me, "Come lie on the ground."

"Why?"

"Will you just trust me? Now lie down on the ground. Please," she begged,

I groaned as I lay down on the ground, "Fine. This is stupid and we're going to get filthy."

"Okay, cool. Now, I want you to scream as loud as you can."

I glared at her, "You've got to be fucking kidding me."

"No. I'm serious. What's the big deal? It's not like anyone can hear us."

She was right, no one else was around.

"On the count of three," Eileen smiled, "One, two, three."

We both yelled as loud as we could. Our sound echoed for miles across the badlands. After screaming, I felt relieved, as if all my worries were suddenly released from me.

"You were right, that did feel good."

Eileen smiled, "What's your ex-boyfriend's name again?"

I frowned, "Arthur. Why do you ask?"

"Tell Arthur what you really think of him."

I looked over at her and started to giggle.

"This is dumb."

"No, it's not. Come on. Consider it free therapy," she said.

"Arthur! You are a lying, cheating, fucking asshole, and I hope you get erectile dysfunction," I yelled.

We both burst out laughing uncontrollably as my voice echoed throughout the land. Suddenly, a park ranger's jeep stopped a few feet beside us and we both jumped up. My cheeks instantly went red from embarrassment.

"Excuse me Ma'am. I heard two women screaming and wondered if everything was ok," said the park ranger.

He looked to be in his early thirties, balding, frumpy, and not attractive.

"Yes sir, everything is AOK.," Eileen chirped.

We burst out laughing while walking back to the car and drove off into the sunset.

*** ***

We had already been on the road for two days and not once had we slept in a normal bed. I wondered how much longer I could keep this up before Eileen would say something. I looked over at her as she was staring out the window onto the highway in complete darkness, minus the occasional bright yellow hazard signs.

"Lily. That's the sixth deer crossing sign in the last hour," she pointed out.

"Really? I didn't notice," I lied.

"Is there anything you want to tell me?"

"No. Why do you ask?" I said.

"You're not short on money, are you? I mean it's okay if you are. If you need to borrow money or something just let me know. Is that why you don't want to stop anywhere and stay in a hotel?"

"No. I have no problem staying at a hotel," I replied.

I hated lying to her. The truth is, I had no money, but I didn't want to borrow any from her. I've always provided for myself and felt guilty asking to borrow money from anyone no matter who they were. I only had five hundred dollars left on my credit card, I knew that wouldn't last long. This stretch of deserted highway I could tell was making Eileen uneasy. She kept looking out the window nervously, as if she had a bad feeling driving all night was going to cause us trouble. I pretended not to notice all the deer crossing signs as the car sped past them.

"That's the seventh deer crossing sign! We have to get off the road before we get hurt," she squealed.

"Okay, no problem. I'll look on my side for a decent hotel and you look on yours."

I slowed the car down as we cruised the highway, desperate to find a place to stay. I had no clue where we were and no desire to ask Eileen to pull out the map, considering the state she was in. The first town we saw, I exited off the highway. This shouldn't have been called a town at all. There was nothing suitable in sight, only one run down gas station, and one old looking restaurant attached to a seedy motel. I sped off, back onto the highway, much to Eileen's dismay, but there was no way I was staying there.

By the time we hit the next town, it was three in the morning.

"Lily! There's one over there," yelled Eileen.

I stopped the car and looked over to my left. A deteriorating, red sign with neon arrows, pointed to the entrance of a motel. The letter O and T were burnt out, reading as *Mel*. An orange and white colored Volkswagen type, hippie van and a rusted nineteen seventies white Pontiac Buick were the only cars parked out front. Besides the mountainside resting behind the motel, nothing else was in clear sight.

I gave Eileen a distained look, "You have got to be

kidding."

"What's wrong with it?"

"What's right with it?"

She rolled her eyes, "It's three in the morning. I'm tired. Let's just suck it up, we can't be picky."

"Fine, but you're coming with me to check in," I said.

We got out of the car and cautiously walked over to the main entrance. Almost on cue, a pack of coyotes began howling in the distance like high-pitched, screaming children, sending shivers down my spine. Instinctively, we both grabbed each other's arm tightly as we continued to approach the motel entrance. Once inside, there wasn't a soul in sight. Their interior décor looked like it was from the seventies. The lobby had all wood paneling with a sand colored shag rug, a few armchairs were placed in front of the desk, with paisley turquoise cushions, a stainless steel commercial sized ashtray filled with used cigarettes sat next to the chairs, and a small desk with pamphlets was nestled in the corner. The door marked management was locked, so I rang the bell on the desk and we waited.

"Ah! For fuck sake," moaned a voice that seemed to be coming from behind the door.

A series of footsteps climbing what sounded like a

set of stairs got louder and louder behind the door. Suddenly the door yanked open. Out from the shadows came a man with a shocking face. His big bald head revealed multiple scars that wrapped around his entire skull. His bottom lip was swollen while the top lip was completely gone, revealing three large dog like front teeth. His nose was crooked and completely off center, when I looked up directly into his black beady little eyes chills ran down my spine. Eileen gave me a quick look of terror and we ran outside, screaming at the top of our lungs. The sound of the coyotes was even louder than before.

"What the hell is that noise?" I yelled.

Eileen looked over and saw a pack of coyotes rushing toward us.

"Get in the car, get in the car," she shouted.

I quickly turned the car key into the lock but it wouldn't turn. Oh, my God, this is just like in the horror movies.

I panicked and started yelling, "It won't open."

The coyotes were getting closer to the car.

"Lily! Do something or we're going to die," shouted Eileen.

I stopped dead in my tracks as the coyotes closed in. Opening my purse, I whipped out my bottle of Dolce &

Gabbana perfume and sprayed it in the coyotes' direction. As they slowly backed up, I threw the entire bottle of perfume at them and began charging toward them, shouting and waving my arms frantically like a crazy person. As the perfume bottle smashed to the ground the coyotes ran back up the mountain in fear. I calmly walked backed to the car and miraculously the door opened.

"Drive," yelled Eileen once we were inside.

"You don't have to tell me twice."

The car engine roared as I put it into overdrive. Rocks and dust shot out from behind us as we sped back onto the highway, into the darkness.

"That was incredible! You handled those coyotes like a pro," said Eileen.

"Thanks, Eileen. Those fuckers cost me a bottle of expensive perfume," I shrugged, "Oh, well, I never really liked the stuff anyway."

We both gave a sigh of relief and went back to staring out the window, looking for the nearest motel to spend the night in. We earned a night of rest and relaxation. We deserved to find a comfy bed to put our heads down on, and, for a moment, to forget all our worries.

CHAPTER NINE
Changes

Three days later, we finally arrived in North Vancouver just in time for winter. This part of the city felt like the entire suburb was under one big bubble, it was heavily populated with dense forestry and wildlife. The pine trees were towering down from the mountains you could see in the distance. A sense of déjà vu came over me as I parked the car; yet, I couldn't quite put my finger on what exactly it was.

"Whoo-hoo! We made it!"

I sat there in absolute silence.

"Lily. Are you okay," Eileen asked, coming down from her excitement.

"I'm fine, just tired from all that driving. Why don't you go inside? I'll join you in a minute," I said.

"Okay, but don't take too long," Eileen replied as

she got out of the car, grabbed her bags and went inside the house.

Then it finally hit me; Vancouver looked exactly like Huntsville, except with mountains. I began to cry. I couldn't believe I'd drove five days to be somewhere that looked like the place I never wanted to see again. I picked up my cell phone from the dashboard and called the only person I knew would care.

"Hello. Lily? Is that you? It's two in the morning for God's sake."

Hearing my mother's voice only made it worse and the tears started flowing even harder.

"What's wrong, Lily?"

"I've made a terrible mistake," I cried.

"What did you do? Lily, are you in trouble? Are you in jail?"

"No, Mom. I'm not in jail, but you might as well call Vancouver that. It looks so much like Huntsville," I said

"But you hated it there," said my mom.

"Exactly. I'm coming home," I whined.

"Now just a minute, young lady. You drove all the way to Vancouver and it hasn't even been a day. Don't you think you should give it a fair chance?"

"It's just that Huntsville was so boring and there was nothing to do there. It was so depressing, Mom. I don't want to relive that ever again," I cried.

"Lily, I want you to stay out there for at least six months, if by then you still don't like it then you can come home. I know it's going to be tough at first but trust me, everything will work out," said my mom.

"But, I don't know anyone here," I said.

"Well that's your fault for driving all the way out there. Speaking of that, actually, there is someone you know."

"And who would that be?" I asked in a sarcastic tone.

"You got a letter a few days ago, from Jamie. I opened it for you since you had already left."

"Mom! That was my mail. I don't open your letters," I said.

"Do you want me to tell you what it says or not?"

"Yes. Please,"

"Now let me see. Dear Lily, it's been a long time, blah blah blah, how are you, blah blah blah. Ah. Here it is. Jamie says his tree-cutting job paid off. He's working full time in Vancouver. He left a telephone number and address. You want it?"

"Um yea, obviously. I desperately need to see a familiar face. Just a second," I said. Searching through my purse, I grabbed a pen and some scrap paper and wrote down the info.

"Thanks Mom. I love you," I said.

"You take care of yourself now," said my mother. Once we hung up, I wiped the tears from my eyes, fixed up my makeup, and went inside the house.

*** ***

Eileen and I spent the entire day looking at apartments. Each time we found a decent place, I'd find an excuse not to get it by pointing out something wrong with it. Finally, the last apartment we saw was perfect. It was in a good location, cheap rent, spacious rooms; there wasn't a single fault I could come up with.

"I don't care what you say, Lily. You have to admit this place is amazing," Eileen said as we stood in the middle of the empty apartment.

"It's ok, I guess."

"Ha! That's the first time all day I haven't heard you say something critical. That's it then; let's take it, let's sign the papers," Eileen cheered.

The landlord took us down to his office and handed

us the lease. I looked it over carefully and started shaking.

Eileen noticed and placed her hand on my shoulder before saying, "Lily, what's wrong?"

I looked over at the landlord, "Do you mind giving us a minute?"

The landlord got up and waited outside the office.

"Eileen, there's something I've been meaning to tell you."

"What's up?"

"This lease says it's for a year. I can't commit to a year of living out here. The truth is, I've been miserable since the moment we arrived," I said.

"Why didn't you say something?"

"I guess, I didn't want to screw you over and leave you without a roommate. I already feel bad for driving all this way with you and wasting your time. You're honestly such a nice person but I just can't do this with you. I'm sorry. I hope you're not mad. I hope you can understand."

I couldn't look at her, but I knew that those eyes were analyzing every visible inch of me. She took a deep breath and said nothing; nervously, looking over the lease.

"So, what are you going to do now?"

"I don't know. Give me a few days to think it over then I promise I will be on my way, wherever that is."

The rest of the car ride home was done in silence. I felt so embarrassed and ashamed. I knew no words could fix this mess I was in, only actions. I could tell Eileen was super pissed at me so I offered to buy her family some groceries. She accepted my offer.

When I made it to the grocery store, it was almost ten at night and the place was empty. As I pushed the cart down the empty aisles, I felt like I was in a drug-induced daze. None of the products on the shelves made any sense. I must have pushed the cart down the same aisle multiple times. It seemed like loneliness followed me everywhere. All I wanted was that feeling of belonging somewhere, anywhere. In the next aisle was a couple, quietly holding hands and kissing. Seeing how happy they were made me feel even more alone. I missed that affection. I hated not having love in my life. I couldn't stand looking at the two of them anymore so I waltzed over to the next aisle.

Suddenly, the grocery store music changed to the song, Here *Comes the Bride*. An attractive man, dressed in a Tux, grabbed me by my arm. I looked down and noticed I was wearing a white wedding dress. As we proceeded down the aisle the shopping cart I was pushing turned into a beautiful bouquet of wild flowers. The closer we got to the end of the aisle the more everything came in focus. The grocery cashier was now wearing a priest's uniform with a red apron tied around his waist. Once we reached the grocery conveyor belt, we stopped and stared into each other's eyes.

"If anyone has a reason as to why these two should not be married, please speak now or forever hold your peace," said the priest.

As I'm on my tippy toes, reaching up to kiss the groom, I felt a repeated light tap on my back.

"Hey. Hey. Lady. Are you okay?"

I whipped around and instantly came out of my daydream to see Martha standing there with a shocked expression on her face.

"Oh, my God. Lily. Is that you? You were out of it there for a minute. What on earth are you doing here?"

Martha was an old high school friend. She used to party with me and some of my other Huntsville friends back in the day. It was strange seeing her in a business suit, with a crisp button up shirt, looking so formal.

Her shoulder length, brown hair went well with her conservative clean-cut look. Martha's big, wide, brown eyes and enormous smile was exactly what I needed to see. It was warm and welcoming. She was always one of those overly perky, energetic, happy girls.

"To be honest, Martha, I have no idea what I'm doing here. I drove out to Vancouver to try and find something new in my life, but instead, it seems like I'm back at square one," I admitted.

She frowned, "Where are you staying?"

"At a friend's place, but I have to be out in a few days."

"If you need a place to stay for a while, until you figure things out, you're welcome to stay with me," she suggested.

She was my savior that day. I still can't believe I ran into her. I must have a guardian angel looking out for me.

A few days later, I said *goodbye* to Eileen and *hello* to Martha. It turns out, Martha went to law school and now works as a clerk at a reputable law firm. She occasionally held work parties at her place and of course I had no choice but to attend. Living in a new city was hard enough, socializing with a room filled with lawyers, clerks, court reporters, private investigators, and numerous others in the same industry was even more intimidating. All they talked about were cases, their boss being an asshole, and who was fucking who at work. As I sat there on Martha's couch, sipping my *Grey Goose* vodka mixed with diet Coke, I listened intensely to the stories about some of the criminals they were defending, but the conversation I found most fascinating were a couple of lawyers debating the myth that all lawyers were liars. The gist of the conversation entailed the final agreement that it is a lawyer's job to manipulate the system, find loopholes, to do whatever they had to do, no matter how ruthless it seemed, to best represent their client. Considering the last two boyfriends I had, I felt uncomfortable being surrounded by professional liars and cheats. The only bonus from hanging around this crowd was their excellent taste in food and alcohol, each party was stocked with nothing but the very best vodkas, champagne, wines, and liqueurs. As I got up to pour myself another drink, Martha came into the kitchen.

"Lily, there's someone I want you to meet," Martha said as she playfully dragged me into the living room.

"Lily, this is Eric. He's a private investigator that our company sometimes uses."

The first thing I noticed about Eric were his light blue eyes. His stare reminded me of one of those seductive models you see on a poster advertising men's cologne where the guy's intense stare makes you feel like he's looking right at you and wants to ravish you whole. His light blue colored, V-neck sweater, was tightly fitted showing off his toned chest. His black dress pants were slim cut, which made it obvious he was fit and frequented the gym. Finally, a guy who knew how to dress, even his dress shoes were stylish, and immaculate. You could tell this was a man who thought through his appearance very well, any sensible woman would be all over him in a second.

"Pleasure to meet you," said Eric as we shook hands. His grip was firm and tight. Out of all the men in the room, he was the only one who peaked my interest.

"So, Lily, what is it that you do for a living?"

"I just got here. I'm job hunting now since I'm new in town," I answered.

"Where are you from?"

"Huntsville, Mississauga, Georgetown, Ontario sums it up, I guess," I laughed.

"How long have you been in Vancouver?"

"What is this? Twenty-one questions?"

"Sorry. Force of habit," he said with an added smile. His teeth were perfectly straight and glistening white. We talked for the rest of the night, making small talk until finally, he had enough glasses of wine in him to grow some balls.

"Listen, Lily, I really enjoyed talking with you this evening," he said.

I couldn't help but smile. It was refreshing talking to a man with manners, even if his conversation was a bit dull. He talked mostly about how much better the weather was in B.C. compared to Toronto, and other topics that seemed pointless to me, then finally, he made his move, he pulled out a small rectangular stainless steel business card holder.

"Here's my card. If you need to reach me, just give me a call. Perhaps we can have lunch sometime this week," he suggested.

He was so prim, and proper, I liked his polite demeanor. Whoever brought him up did a good job.

"That would be nice," was my response.

Eric drew out his black notepad with such precision, he looked like a cowboy drawing his gun.

"What's the best number to reach you at?"

I grabbed the notepad from his hand, took his pen, and wrote down my telephone number.

"Thank you very much. I will be in contact with you in the next few days. You have a good night," he nodded, before standing up.

I watched him do up his navy blue trench coat, put on a black fedora, and walk out the door. It was a strange exit.

Oh well, at least I finally felt a tinge of excitement about being out there. Perhaps Eric was the reason I came to Vancouver. Maybe he would finally be the guy that I'd been looking for all these years.

Before I went to bed, my final thoughts for the night were how much I missed the security of my home and being close to my family.

CHAPTER TEN
Private Dick

It took Eric four days to call and ask me out.

He arrived at the door wearing the exact same outfit as before; except, he had on an olive-green-colored V-neck sweater this time.

I stepped out the door, he took me by the arm, walked me over to his car, opened my door, then closed it behind me.

I guess chivalry wasn't dead.

His car was spotless, a black two-seater sports car that looked expensive and brand new. I certainly could get used to this.

Eric started the car, the engine purred like a cat.

"Nice ride," I said.

"Thanks. It's a Nissan, the V-6 engine has a lot of

power, I hope you like going fast. I chose black so that my car won't be as noticeable on the street."

"You sure are thorough at making decisions," I half chuckled.

"In my line of work, you must be to stay alive," said Eric.

I peered out the window at the stars in the sky. The car had picked up generous speed and was traveling away from the downtown, into the wilderness.

"Where are you taking me?"

"Now, that would ruin the surprise. Don't all women like surprises?"

"Yes, of course I love surprises. It's not like I'd know the place though Eric, I've only been out here two weeks, silly."

Looking around at the car's interior I noticed it contained several buttons, dials, and display screens, it was mesmerizing. Underneath the dashboard was a large black colored car phone.

"Does this thing actually work," I asked.

"Yeah. Why do you ask?"

"It looks like something from the eighties," I replied.

"You making fun of my car?"

I giggled, "No, sorry I didn't mean it like that. Although you do realize pocket size cell phones exist right."

He glared, "Well it came installed in the car, so I just left it there, not everything old should be discarded you know."

He had a point, I felt stupid.

I had to figure out how to turn this date around, it didn't seem to be going well at all.

I picked up the car phone, and said, "Hello, I'd like to order a pizza with mushroom, and pepperoni."

"I get it, sometimes I get a bit too serious, you're cute Lily."

Then he put his hand on my knee and I leaned over to put my head on his shoulder.

That put everything at ease. The car kept climbing higher and higher up the mountain, the road was narrow with several twists and turns, it made me nervous how fast he was going around some of the corners.

"So, what's the big deal with a V-6 engine," I asked.

Big mistake.

Eric peered over at me with a sly smile, put his hand on the clutch, and the car's wheels made a screeching sound as he sped up. I shouldn't have asked. I was shitting my pants.

When we finally reached our destination, I was glad the ride was over.

The car pulled up to a five-story tall building on stilts, encased with glass. It looked stunning with the mist flowing off the mountaintop that blended in with the snow scape.

I followed Eric inside the building marked, *Grouse Mountain*. The interior was very cozy and welcoming. Two large intricately carved oak pillars sat at the entrance with oak railings running along a spiral staircase in the center of the room. Eric walked over to the lobby attendant, handed his car keys to the valet service, then checked our winter coats.

"Enjoy your evening, Mister Peterson," said the female attendant.

He seemed important.

He must come here often, I thought.

Eric took me by the arm and slowly walked me up the stairs to the restaurant. Light jazz music was playing in the background. The hostess greeted us with a warm smile.

"Mister Peterson, welcome back. Care for your usual table," asked the young lady.

"No thank you, Alice. Tonight, is rather special. I believe I have a reservation, a table for two, by the window," Eric replied.

"Yes of course. Please, follow me this way," she smiled.

We followed her over to our table that was angled toward the glass window, giving us a perfect, scenic view. The table linen was crisp white with matching napkins. The oak, wing backed chairs gave off a feeling of sheer elegance. Eric pulled my chair out from under the table. As I sat down I couldn't help but admire the spectacular view through the tall glass windows, it reminded me of Deerhurst. The restaurant was lit with candles, giving the entire room a warm romantic ambience. It seemed to further compliment the wonderful view outside, especially the tall green Douglas firs that surrounded the entire building.

"This place is beautiful," I remarked.

"I'm glad you like it, Lily," Eric smiled.

We both stared into each other's eyes, I felt my attraction for him grow stronger, it was a moment of intimacy that I hadn't felt since we'd first met. Our waiter, who looked to be in his mid-thirties approached the table. His name was Charles, how fitting for a fancy restaurant like this.

"Good evening. Welcome to the Observatory restaurant at Grouse Mountain. It's a pleasure to have you back Mr. Peterson. Can I start you off with a beverage; perhaps, a nice bottle of wine?"

"Yes. I'd like a bottle of the nineteen ninety-six Château Léoville-Barton red Bordeaux," said Eric.

"I'm not much of a wine drinker, if you don't mind I'd like a Grey Goose and cranberry in a short glass please," I said.

Charles nodded, "I'll be back in a moment with your drinks."

Another server placed a basket of warm French bread, with a side of herb butter, on the table. The texture of the bread was soft and the crust was not too hard, just the perfect amount of firmness. Buttering the bread gave off a faint odor of chives. It melted in my mouth and was purely divine.

"Mind if I ask you a question?"

I looked up from my delicious treat to see Eric gazing at me.

"Only if it doesn't turn into an interrogation," I laughed.

"Grey Goose vodka mixed with cranberry juice

seems like such a waste," he stated.

I frowned, "What do you mean?"

"Grey Goose is a premium vodka, why ruin its natural flavor by dousing it with juice? Perhaps you are better off mixing it with a lesser quality vodka since you won't notice that much difference," said Eric.

"I guess the reason is because I like the taste. Take for example a lesser quality vodka like a Smirnoff or Absolut. Mixing that together in most cocktails, I find it tastes like rubbing alcohol. Grey Goose mixed with cranberry tastes like cranberry with a subtle kick to it. Good vodka is smooth, and mild, almost like water. So, that's why I drink Grey Goose," I replied pointblank.

"Fair enough. In fact, I'm impressed. I've never met a woman before who knows her alcohol as well as you do," he smiled.

"Well, I used to be a cocktail waitress at a five-star resort, guess I picked up a few things," I said with a smile.

Looking at the menu, I was unsure what to order. It was my first time eating in a fancy restaurant. Everything seemed too exotic for me. Something needs to be said about keeping food simple.

Charles returned to our table and asked, "Are you ready to place your order?"

"Yes. Lily, if you don't mind I'll order for the both us," said Eric.

"Um, okay," I said.

"We'll have the usual."

Charles nodded, before grabbing the menus, "Excellent choice, enjoy your evening."

As he walked away, I noticed Eric swirling his wine glass and taking small gulps.

"Thanks, Eric. I wasn't sure what to order. I've never heard of any of these dishes. It's as if you read my mind," I admitted.

"Don't worry, after a few more visits, you'll get the hang of it. It's great being a regular somewhere. It comes with perks and special treatment. The staff gets to know exactly what your tastes are, they make excellent recommendations, and the chef will make you anything you want if you don't see anything you like on the menu."

"Yes, I noticed that. It seems everyone here knows your name. Do you bring all your dates here?"

I was joking, of course. Actually, no I wasn't, I really did want to know the answer. I hoped that Eric wasn't the playboy type that wined and dined a harem of women.

"No. I'm usually on my own for the most part

except, on a few rare occasions when I bring prospective clients for lunch. In fact, I haven't been out on a date in over six months. Too busy with work," was his honest answer.

Just then, Charles came back with two bowls and placed them on the table. Another server stood at the opposite side, grating thin slices of fresh Parmesan cheese on top of each bowl of soup, and then cracking just a dash of black pepper from his mill.

"What is it?" I asked.

"Try it and find out," said Eric.

I scooped a large amount of the thick red liquid into my mouth. The texture reminded me of a homemade thick salsa.

"What do you taste?"

"Tomatoes, wait, one more sip, whoa that's spicy, there definitely is some sort of kick to it, jalapeño pepper and onion, I think. Whatever it is, it's delicious," I said.

"Exquisite taste buds, Lily. It's a roasted tortilla and tomato soup with jalapeño pepper and onion. You missed the hint of fresh garlic and smoked paprika but for a first guess you did surprisingly well," said Eric.

As pretentious as Eric was at times, this little guessing game was fun. Not often did I get the chance to pretend to be a food connoisseur, and apparently, I was good at it.

"So, Mr. Detective, what made you want to become a private eye anyway," I asked.

"If I tell, I must kill you," he laughed.

"I promise, I will take your secret to the grave," I smiled.

"No, it's embarrassing and you're going to laugh at me when I tell you," said Eric.

"I won't. I promise."

"Okay, I trust you, I think. Have you ever heard of the TV show, *MacGyver*?"

"Doesn't ring a bell," I said.

He gasped, "Are you serious? That show was a classic."

"Sorry. I didn't watch much TV growing up. We moved to a small town, only one TV and three channels to share between all of us, my Dad usually won. It was Hockey Night in Canada every Saturday night at our house."

"Well anyway, the show was about a guy who made up all kinds of devices to get out of sticky situations. I thought it would be cool to have a job like that," he smiled, clearly excited just by thinking of it all.

"Oh, now I remember. Wasn't the show called Knight Rider?"

"No. That was the one with the high-tech car," said Eric.

"Oops. Sorry. Please continue," I said.

"I was in New York and stumbled across a store that sold a bunch of surveillance equipment and gadgets that private investigators use. I thought, 'Hey, if I was a P.I. I'd get to use all that stuff'. It would almost be like being a real-life *MacGyver*. Plus, who doesn't love helping people put away the bad guys. That's when I decided to become a private investigator," he informed me.

I couldn't help it, I burst out laughing. Maybe it was the alcohol.

"You promised that you wouldn't laugh," he frowned.

"Sorry, that was just adorable, I couldn't help it, you looked so serious and cute telling your story."

I was starting to like this guy.

Charles interrupted us with another course, it was perfect timing, this time he dropped off a Waldorf salad.

"We'll have another round of drinks," Eric ordered.

Charles nodded and walked away.

"You sure you want another bottle of wine, Eric?

How exactly are we getting home? I don't get in cars with a drunk driver."

He chuckled, "You worry too much, Lily. Everything has been taken care of."

We sat there eating our salad in awkward silence. For some reason, hearing Eric say those words got me nervous and excited at the same time. I barely knew this guy and I didn't want to do something I would regret. Not knowing what he had planned, I figured I might as well enjoy myself and started drinking more than usual. The worst that could happen is I'd have to call a cab.

"I think that is very noble of you, wanting to be a private detective. So, what has been your most difficult case? Was it a murder investigation, a missing person, or let me guess, a husband cheating?"

"No. I specialize in insurance fraud and workers comp claims. Whenever a company suspects an employee is not actually as sick or injured as they claim, that's when they call me and I follow them. I also specialize in infidelity investigations," said Eric.

"Oh, that sounds like dirty work," I said.

"Well, maybe, but somebody's got to do it. It may as well be me getting paid for it," said Eric. I think I offended him so I told him I wasn't exactly living my dream life either. My dream was to become an actress, and I was a far cry from that waiting tables for a living.

"I have an idea. Since you seem so interested in what I do maybe you can come along with me on my next case," said Eric.

"Are you asking me to go spy on someone with you?" I said.

"Don't say it like that. Come on, it will be fun," said Eric.

"Let's just see how tonight goes, okay?" I said.

The rest of the meal consisted of guessing games between Eric and I as to what each ingredient was in each course. The main dish was a delicate piece of arctic char with a side of acorn squash, creamed spinach and pistachio orange vinaigrette. By this time, I've already had a few too many Grey Goose so I settled on water for the rest of the meal to sober me up a bit. When dessert came, I could barely move I was so full. I gave into the temptation out of curiosity as to what house made French vanilla ice cream tasted like on top of a honey, ginger, cinnamon poached pear, surrounded by pieces of cheesecake topped with mango coulis and a warm maple bourbon sauce. Each bite was like an orgasm in my mouth I highly recommend trying this. After Eric paid for the meal, we walked outside.

The cold temperature instantly sobered me up, however it did not have the same effect on Mr. P.I. It was entertaining seeing Eric tipsy. He was more fun and relaxed, that made him even more attractive. He tried his best to mask his intoxication; as if he was somehow a lesser person yet his effort to sound sober and in control resulted in some slight slurring of the tongue, making it more obvious he was in fact a little drunk.

"Where to now lover boy," I said mockingly.

Eric looked at his watch then looked at me with a coy smile. We walked in the complete opposite direction of the car toward an empty sky ride terminal.

"What the hell are we doing here?" I asked Eric, who paid no attention to my words. He just kept standing there looking at his watch.

"Should be here in just about now," said Eric.

Just then through the winter snow, a red blob slowly appeared in the sky coming up toward the mountain and heading straight for us. Eric walked over to the sky ride attendant and whispered in his ear. The attendant looked over at me and gave Eric a wink. Then they exchanged hands as Eric slipped him a fifty-dollar bill. The sky ride slowly made its way inside the terminal and made a complete stop unloading its passengers. Judging by the size of the sky ride, it could easily hold over thirty people. A large group of people eagerly stood in line behind us as we waited for the attendant to escort us onboard. The attendant went inside the sky ride and whispered something to the operator manning the controls. The operator nodded as the attendant pointed to the two of us. As Eric and I got on sky ride the attendant closed the door, and put the rope back up in front of the line.

"Sorry folks, this one's full," he said. The crowd started cursing profusely and demanding an explanation.

"Take it nice and slow," said Eric.

"You got it," said the operator as he flipped the switch and the car began to move.

"You planned all of this, wow, impressive. What else do you have up your sleeve?" I wondered.

"Come over here Lily. I want to show you something," said Eric.

He walked over to the middle of the car and pointed out the window. It was a view overlooking Vancouver's skyscrapers the twinkling city lights reflected off the Georgia Straight waters, and lit up the night sky.

"Wow. This is amazing Eric," I said.

Eric looked intensely into my eyes putting one arm around my waist and the other carefully behind my neck as he bent in for a soft kiss. I melted into his embrace. This was the ultimate romantic moment. The only thing missing was a ring, and a proposal. He continued to plant soft kisses on my upper lip then moved to the bottom lip. I glanced over at the sky ride operator, to make sure he wasn't watching us. Luckily, the controls were facing the other direction and he was turned away from us. I closed my eyes relished the moment, and lost myself in Eric's kisses. His hand moved its way down from my waist and onto my butt, as he pulled me in closer I could feel how hard he was getting. As our legs rubbed together the tip of Eric's tongue slid around my mouth sending sensual shivers down my spine. The more our bodies rubbed together the deeper our kisses became. If it wasn't for the sky ride operator I swear we would have probably had sex right, then and there. We broke our embrace when we heard a terrible screeching sound that startled both of us. The sky ride had reached the end, and was docking into the terminal. Eric grabbed my hand and walked us off the sky ride. He put his arm around my shoulder, and continued kissing me as we walked toward the building in front of us.

"You are so beautiful Lily," said Eric.

I smiled, and kissed him on the cheek. Eric stopped walking as we approached a large stretch limousine that was parked in front of us. The driver got out, opened the door for us and we climbed in. Inside the limo was a bucket of champagne. At this point I didn't care where we were going all I wanted to do was make out with him, which is exactly what we did the entire ride over. I had to stop Eric from almost tearing my clothes off. I knew I shouldn't even be considering having sex with him on our first date, especially not in a car. I deserved better than that. Eric grabbed the bucket of champagne and we got out of the vehicle. I was so taken by this amazing night, and Eric, I didn't even notice we had stopped in front of a gorgeous resort, it had to be a five-star hotel judging by how elegant the lobby was, and how formal the doorman was dressed.

As the elevator doors closed, Eric pinned me against the wall and started kissing my neck. When we arrived onto the top floor, we got out of the elevator and walked into the penthouse suite. Eric closed the door and poured us each a glass of champagne.

"You hungry?" asked Eric.

I said yes, even though I was stuffed like a pig. I didn't want to ruin what his next surprise might be. Sure enough, a minute later room service arrived with a plate of a dozen chocolate covered strawberries. Each strawberry was drizzled with both white and dark chocolate swirls.

They were delicious. As I nibbled on the strawberries, and sipped my champagne, Eric got up and turned on the fireplace. Even though it was electric, the flame and charcoal looked so real, it made the ambience even more romantic. Eric went over to a panel on the wall and pushed a button. Instantly, "I don't see nothing wrong, with a little bump and grind," blasted through the speakers.

Maybe it was my fault for believing in stereotypes, but I was a little surprised at his choice in music, I expected him to put on something classical, or jazz. Satisfied with the look on my face of pure delight, Eric walked over and sat beside me on the brown leather couch. He put the last remaining strawberry into my mouth, as he took a bite on the other end; he gently bit down on my bottom lip. His hands slowly made their way across my breast. I grabbed the back of his head and gently massaged it, slowly pulling him into me. There was only one way this evening was going to end, and that was us in bed together. I was in my thirties, we were grown adults, did I have to play hard to get? These moments were few and far between, I wanted to just go for it, to feel alive again. I was fully aware of my own immortality due to living with my parents and seeing these two strong vibrant people who still had all their mental youth deteriorate physically as their bodies started to give out on them. I wanted to be kissed, I wanted to be in a man's embrace, I wanted to have amazing sex. I'm sick of that translating into being a bad girl. Sex is an amazing pleasure we get to experience here on earth, yet society has twisted it into something dirty.

Long periods of loneliness also played a part in me choosing to live in the moment. I had only been out with this guy once and already he was about to get in my pants. I knew per society; I wasn't supposed to let it get this far. I could blame it on the chemistry between us; or blame it on the alcohol, or maybe I believed someone was mature enough to see me as the good person that I was, and I decided to say fuck society and its rules. Life is too short; I just decided to not give a damn about being judged for what I was about to do. I always thought the double standard that men can sleep around with tons of women but a woman must play the virgin no matter how old she is, was bullshit. I was all alone in a new place feeling home sick, it's normal to want a little affection, and comfort. Besides, this was the best way to get over Arthur.

Eric's well-manicured hands were inside my lace panties. He knew how to touch me and it was driving me wild. I could feel his erection digging into me. I slid Eric's V-neck sweater off and was surprised to see exactly how toned his upper body was. Eric gently rubbed my clit in a slow circular motion. My hands were spread out gripping the sofa as tight as I could, so I didn't roll right off it. Eric removed his hand to slowly undo his dress pants.

"Don't stop," I moaned.

I wasn't ready to have sex, I wanted to delay it if I could hold out. I was trying to be good. Shocked at this response Eric quickly put his hands back inside my underwear until I was completely soaked. I couldn't take it anymore. I wanted him so bad. I got up, took his pants off and pulled down his white Calvin Klein underwear. His penis was beautiful; it was the most perfect penis I'd ever seen, long, thick, hard, flawless smooth skin. Eric quickly pulled my shirt over my head, and undid my bra with one hand. I was impressed. He started sucking on my nipples. Eric slid me off the couch, and placed me on top of him beside the fireplace. Then he rolled me sideways so that he was on top, and grabbed my left leg pressing my thigh up against his waist, thrusting himself deep inside me. We made love for hours, until we passed out from exhaustion, on the white bear skin rug in front of the fireplace.

Chapter Eleven
The Pursuit of Reality

I woke up the next morning to an empty room filled with nothing but the sound of my own pounding headache. I frantically searched through my purse for a painkiller, grabbed my clothes, and took a hot shower. When I got out of the bathroom, Eric was comfortably seated on the sofa, reading the newspaper.

"I thought you had left," I breathed.

"No. Went for my morning jog. Did you know everyone should exercise at least three times a week?"

"Yes, I remember reading that somewhere. You know, Eric, you could have left me a note," I replied.

Eric sat there, staring at his newspaper in a sleepy stupor.

"Huh? Did you say something?"

"I said you could have left a note," I repeated.

"Right, sorry about that. Next time," he paused, "Oh by the way, I took the liberty of ordering us some breakfast."

Suddenly there was a knock on the door.

"Ah. That must be it."

Eric let in two room service staff members and promptly gave them a tip before whisking them away. An assortment of croissants, muffins, and bread rolls lay in a basket, next to a plate of fresh preserves, consisting of strawberry jam, marmalade, and honey. Two glasses of freshly squeezed orange juice sat on either side of the large plates. There was also a large pot of coffee, thank God. I poured myself a cup immediately.

After lifting the round, silver plate cover, I revealed thick homemade French toast with a side of bacon, sausage, home fries, and fresh fruit. Eric's dish contained a single poached egg, fresh fruit and a dry English muffin. The fact that Eric was still treating me great the morning after was promising. After we finished eating, we gathered our things and he drove me back to Martha's around noon.

When I arrived, the place was in a total mess with drug paraphernalia scattered all over the room and a mountain of cocaine sitting on top of the glass table in the living room. There was a naked man on the couch and used condoms everywhere. Being a small-town girl, the only drugs I'd been exposed to was marijuana. I felt disgusted with the scene in front of me. I was concerned about the amount of cocaine that was just sitting there, left out for the entire world to see. I never did cocaine, but I knew of the potentially harmful and addictive effects it had on others.

Martha and one of her friends were just finishing doing a line when they looked up at me.

"Hey Lily, how was your date?"

"It was nice. What is all this?"

I gestured around the room and Martha looked around as if it as her first time noticing it too.

She laughed, before wiping the leftovers from under her nose, "Seeing how you were out last night, me and the girls had a little wild party. You want to do a rail?"

I shot her a look of disapproval and said, "No thanks, I'm still a bit tired from last night. I think I'll just lie down for a while."

I walked into my bedroom and closed the door. My bed was a mess; it obviously had been used for God knows what. I couldn't say much. I needed a place to stay. I felt sick to my stomach at the thought of staying there though. I should've never left my parents' home. I have never lived around drugs and I certainly didn't want to start now. Resisting the urge to call my mother, I decided to call Eric instead. Last night had to mean something to him. I went on a hunch that he was into me and would want to see me again.

*** ***

"Are you okay?" he asked once I had gotten him on the phone.

"I don't know. I really want to move back home, but I can't afford to even leave B.C. until I save up enough money," I said.

"If you need some money I can help."

"No, I can't do that. I appreciate it, Eric, but borrowing money is the last thing I want to do," I admitted.

There was silence on the phone. My guess is he wasn't use to women turning down money, he was speechless. I didn't want any handouts and I honestly wasn't interested in Eric's offer because I knew there was a chance I couldn't pay him back. I would have felt like shit if that happened. I didn't want any feelings of regret going on in my life; I already had enough past mistakes to deal with.

"You can stay with me if you like," he suggested.

"I can't do that either," I replied.

"Yes, you can. It's easy. Either take money from me to get yourself back home, or move in with me until you get yourself back on your feet. You can decide to stay or leave then. The choice is yours," said Eric.

He instantly came to my rescue. He told me to pack up all my stuff, put it in my car, and he'd be there to get me within the hour.

I was out of Martha's drug house and into Eric's downtown loft by nightfall. Eric lifted my suitcase down his black ash colored staircase that led into the living room. The level of cleanliness was astounding creating an almost sterile feel to the place. The gray concrete walls and wood ceiling gave it a contemporary industrial modern look. The color scheme in his living room consisted of grays, blacks, whites and beige. It looked like a design team decorated it. I walked over to the sofa and sat down. Eric was a minimalist believing less was more. His concept was that furniture stands out better when you have less clutter in a room. I liked his style. His place was perfectly put together; it looked like one of the show rooms at Ikea. If only he was a little more emotional and less like a computer that had all the answers. I looked at my watch and it was almost six thirty in the evening, I was starving.

"Eric. I don't mean to be a bother, I haven't had anything to eat since this morning, do you feel like grabbing a bite, I'm a little hungry," I asked sheepishly.

"Of course, how rude of me, just sit right down and relax Lily. I'll whip you up something in no time," said Eric.

I watched him almost on command walk right into the kitchen; his place was open concept so I could see him cooking in the kitchen from where I sat in the living room. All the appliances were made of stainless steel, and the cabinets were black. A long island served as both a prep station and dining table with a round sink and a large wood cutting board built into the island itself. Four tall black bar stools were positioned at the end of the island. After watching Eric start to prepare dinner, then carefully trim pieces of salmon for over a half an hour, I decide to wander around and be nosey. I started snooping around his place trying to find clues as to exactly what kind of man Eric was. First stop were the open-faced bookshelves filled with old records. The albums that stood out were from Genesis, Annie Lennox and Bad Company.

"Quite the music collection you have there," I said.

"Thank you, Lily. Without music, life would be a mistake. Friedrich Nietzsche said that," Eric replied.

"Oh really? Hmmm," I said half heartedly.

I picked up the Alan Parson Projects album entitled *Eve*. The first song was an instrumental piece called *Lucifer*. It sounded like a theme song an Olympic athlete would use to train to.

"Anything I can do to help?" I asked.

"Sure. You could peel some potatoes if you like," said Eric.

I picked up the peeler and got to work. After peeling my first potato, Eric peered over at me and snatched it out of my hand.

"No, no, no. What on earth are you doing," Eric snapped.

He then proceeded to demonstrate the so-called proper way of peeling a potato, which was moving the peeler in a perfectly circular motion. His angry outburst started to make me wonder if moving in with Eric was such a wise choice after all. The question was, did I want to live with a drug user, or take a chance with a guy who was starting to seem like a Nazi control freak? It's ironic that the song playing in the background was called Lucifer because Eric was starting to seem like the devil and Vancouver was becoming my new hell. What the fuck was I doing here? My instincts kept telling me to pack up and drive back to Toronto. The only thing stopping me was money, and my mother. I knew if I went home now I'd disappoint her. I loved my mother and respected her wishes. I knew she was doing this because she loved me and wanted me to forget about Arthur. Of course, the more I thought about my mother the more I missed her and the rest of my family. Family is family no matter what happens they are always there for you. At least that's how my family was. I had very little money left so I figured I may as well stick it out until I could get myself a stable enough job to move out on my own.

    Deciding it best not to assist master chef Hitler, I went back to exploring his apartment. I wandered into the bedroom scared to death what I might discover underneath his bed, or hidden in his closet. I found out my instincts were dead on when I opened Eric's closet and discovered what was behind those doors, it looked like he was in the military. He had one style of dress pants, the same went for his jeans, V-neck sweaters, and t-shirts. Everything was ironed, perfectly folded, and sorted by color, fit, and style. His boxer briefs were all the same brand and either black or white. Inside the nightstand drawer was a book on sexual positions that help bring a woman to climax, of course written by a man. I flipped to a page that had a Post-it note stuck to it, and found he had bookmarked the same sexual position we attempted the night before. That creeped me out; somehow the sexual positions coming from someone performing what he read in an instructional manual, and not spontaneous in the moment, made me cringe. Not knowing how long I could realistically stay there, I didn't unpack, I decided to leave all my belongings in my suitcase, in the event I had to make a quick exit.

Eric summoned me back into the living room and we sat down to a dinner of pan-fried salmon, mashed potatoes and fresh green beans. I thought it was a bit weird that he wrapped sliced lemons in netting but I said nothing, I didn't want to seem ungrateful. As I lifted the lemon into the air and was about to squeeze it onto my salmon Eric quickly grabbed it, snatched it out of my hand and said, "Let me show you how to properly squeeze a lemon."

He lifted his fork slowly into the air as if I was a child.

"You have to pierce it with your fork first then squeeze it ever so slightly. That way the juices don't spray all over everything," said Eric.

The rest of the dinner I sat there in silence, not wanting to show my anger at his silly little know it all games. I knew at that moment I had no future with this person. He was not the "One" for me. The more instructional he became the less attracted I was to him. Maybe his mannerisms would go over well with other women, someone with low self-esteem perhaps, but they didn't sit well with me. Having confidence is one thing but no one deserves to be treated like an idiot.

We spent the rest of the night watching television.

If our sexual attraction was on the stock market, the value of this stock just crashed. To avoid any advances, he might make in hopes of trying a different page in his book, I pretended to fall asleep on the sofa that night, much to Eric's surprise. The next morning Eric made us breakfast and convinced me to go along with him on a stake out job. I didn't want to go but I was curious what a day in the life of a P.I. entailed. Driving around downtown Vancouver and getting to see the city was fun. Our first stop was a spy tech store that sold a wide variety of surveillance equipment.

To the naked eye the shop looked much like your run of the mill electronics store. There were assorted security cameras carefully fixed along one wall. Underneath these cameras were large boxes that looked like VCR's, I assumed they were some sort of digital recording device. Directly opposite were the more ingenious hidden cameras. Everything from a teddy bear, a tip jar commonly seen at most stores beside the cash register, a functioning clock, tool boxes, a can of pop and even a hidden camera fitted into a business tie. Some of these cameras were hooked up to television monitors inside the store to demonstrate their capabilities. At the same time, they served a double purpose by deterring shoplifters who were warned they were being watched by the sign that stated, 'This store is under surveillance'. It would take a complete moron to attempt stealing anything in this store. Looking at all these devices made me wonder how many times I may have been under surveillance without knowing. The idea of someone else watching my every move made me shiver.

Eric introduced me to the manager of the store, Walter. He was a thick built man in his late forties with a full head of gray hair carefully slicked back, and matching gray mustache. He wore thick-rimmed glasses that suited his oval face quite well. He had a friendly smile, and eyes that radiated a sort of welcoming sensibility about him.

"Eric! Wait till you see what new products I got in store for you," said Walter.

Eric smiled, which was quite a feat since that was the only facial expression I saw him make all day. Walter produced a pair of black sunglasses, and handed them to Eric. He examined the pair of designer sunglasses with smoky colored lenses.

"So? What's the big deal? The lenses are fitted with a hidden camera, am I, right?" asked Eric.

"Try them on and see for yourself," said Walter.

As soon as Eric put them on he jumped back in shock.

"This is incredible. I'll take a pair," said Eric.

I looked over at the two of them waiting for him to include me in what exactly it was he just saw; it was as if I wasn't even there. I felt like a ghost in the room. To stop from being excluded I grabbed a palm sized device with three dials on it, and a LED screen, like what you'd find on a digital calculator, and put it on the counter.

"What's this thing do?" I asked.

I immediately had Walter and Eric's attention. These two practically tackled each other trying to be the one who was going to explain to me, what this thing did.

"That's the pocket lie detector. It analyzes the level of truth in audio statements from video, phone, or even in person," said Walter.

"Sounds neat, how does it work?" I asked.

Walter pulled out the black and white instructional manual and flipped to a diagram with images of apples. If the apple was completely shaded in, they were telling the truth. Likewise, for the screen if the apple showed up on the screen that indicated a percentage of stress levels and how badly they were lying. Finally, if the apple was completely gone and only the core remained it meant that the person was full of shit and rotten to the core. Guess that's why they chose to use an apple as the corresponding illustration. If you ask me, we should all carry one of those in our pockets, especially on a date. Might save us a lot of time wasted on frauds. Eric paid for the sunglasses and lie detector and off we went on our merry way.

*** ***

Forty minutes later, Eric and I were sitting comfortably parked outside what looked like a well-off suburban residential neighborhood in North Vancouver.

"Lily, here's the scoop," said Eric as he passed me a large manila envelope. I untied the red string and took out a large eight by ten black and white photo of an attractive man in his early thirties.

"Subject is known as Frank Parker. Aged thirty-two. Five foot nine with dark brown eyes and black hair. Married to a Sylvia Parker for over five years. Works as a general manager at a local department store. His wife believes he's been cheating on her," said Eric.

I discovered soon enough that sitting in a car for hours on end waiting for something to happen is about as much fun as watching paint dry. There is no way I could ever make it in the private eye business. Eric carefully parked the car about a block away from the targets house to give us an excellent vantage point for surveillance, and escape if we needed to follow him. I watched as Eric picked up a pair of high-powered binoculars and peered into the front window of the house. A pale blue Cadillac Deville was parked in Frank's driveway indicating that he was still at home.

"So, do you think this guy is a cheater?" I asked.

"All the signs are there. Spouse has reported an increase in overtime at work, lower sex drive at home, more time spent at the gym, he's watching what he eats, overly concerned about his appearance, has started dressing more stylish, seems to have completely lost interest in his wife. Those are all the telltale signs someone is cheating. The question is can we prove it? Judging by his habits this guy is careful and extremely smart. I have taps on his cell, and home phone neither has picked up any mysterious calls, or messages. I've been watching this guy for over a week now and I still haven't found any legitimate incriminating evidence to back up what his wife has accused him of. Yet my instincts tell me, this guy is a cheater, I can feel it in my bones." said Eric.

"I'm just curious Eric, how many cases do you get related to cheating?" I asked. Eric let out a laugh.

"I lost track, dozens per year. I read somewhere that thirty percent of all men and women cheat. The problem is that information was based on a survey. It doesn't take a rocket scientist to figure out that most people probably lie about being a cheater. Which means the number is probably double what the magazine poll calculated," said Eric.

For the first time Eric's computer like knowledge came in handy and made for an interesting conversation. We talked about why we think most people cheat. He thought that most were bored at home, or serial cheaters, and couldn't commit to one person. I added that I thought some of it came from people who grew up in broken homes, with parents that didn't show them love, or security. I think that leaves an emptiness that can't be filled by anyone, no matter how much you love them. That was my experience anyway with men that grew up with a stepfather. They all had commitment issues, they were unfaithful, pathological liars, and had no idea how to truly accept, or show love. Then there is always simply giving into the devil's temptation of lust.

Hours later finally there was movement. A male hand anxiously lifted the blind on the window; he seemed to be glaring out impatiently as if he was expecting someone and they were late. I could see why Eric's windows had such a dark tint on them; it wasn't him just trying to be cool after all. A minute later the blinds returned to normal and no other movement was seen for hours once again. Eric pulled out a plastic water bottle with the top cut off.

"What's that for?" I asked.

"It's my urine bottle," said Eric.

"Gross. You're not really going to use that thing in front of me, are you?" I inquired.

"What do you expect me to do, pee in my pants? When you got to go, you got to go," said Eric.

"Can't you just find a bush or something," I said.

"Are you crazy? I can't risk losing sight of the subject to take a leak. That could be the moment he decides to leave. If I lose him an entire day's work is lost," said Eric.

"Do me a favor and hold it in, please," I begged. Eric let out a long sigh as I picked up the binoculars and took a gander at Frank's house.

I saw the door open as Frank walked outside and locked up. He kept looking over his shoulder as if he knew someone was watching him. If Frank were innocent, he sure as hell wouldn't be acting so guilty. I knew I had to catch this sleaze ball. This was for all the guys who ever cheated on me, and for all the innocent women out there that have been betrayed by scumbags like Frank. Call it retribution if you will, this guy was going to pay.

"Eric. He's coming out the door," I yelled.

Eric took out his Canon camera with a zoom lens and began taking photos on burst mode as Frank walked over to his car.

"That's the best you can do, take photos? What's that going to prove?" I yelled.

"Calm down, Lily. This is how the job is done," said Eric.

The Cadillac slid its way onto the road and slowly sped off into the distance.

"He's getting away," I said.

"Here, take the camera and grab a shot if you can," said Eric as he started the car's ignition and began to follow the suspect. I kept my eyes on the car the whole time by using the camera like a pair of binoculars. We were one block away from each other, right on his tail as Frank lead us into the downtown core. As soon as we left the suburbs, it was more difficult to be discrete, the traffic got heavier which meant we had to follow closer to the vehicle and risk being exposed. We were stopped at a red light about five cars behind Frank's.

"Drive closer when it turns green," I said.

"Lily, you have no idea what you're talking about. If the car gets too close we risk being seen," said Eric.

"Oh, grow a pair of balls for Christ sake," I said.

Not wanting to look like a pussy, Eric listened to my command. As soon as the light turned green Eric sped up cutting in between lanes until we were right behind the Cadillac. I took out the camera and grabbed a quick shot. Frank considered his rearview mirror. His eyes glaring back at us gave me the willies.

"Lily what the hell are you doing," yelled Eric.

"What? You said for me to take photos," I barked back.

"Yes, but not when he's a few feet away from us," yelled Eric.

"Now you tell me," I said.

"Quick, duck down," said Eric.

"Why?" I asked.

"Just do it before it's too late," Eric yelled.

"Okay but stop yelling at me," I said.

As soon as I undid my seatbelt and ducked down the light turned green and the sound of tires squealing was heard all around me as the Cadillac zoomed away from us at a high speed.

"I knew it. He's onto us," said Eric.

I watched his hand move onto the clutch as Eric accelerated into second gear. I tried to pop my head up to see what was going on, and make sure Eric's eyes were on the road. Both cars were dangerously swerving in and out of lanes.

"Why is it again I'm ducking?" I asked.

"Just keep down. I will explain later," said Eric.

I frantically held on for dear life as best I could. The faster Eric drove the harder it was for me to stop myself from being bumped around. As I popped my head up I noticed in the distance the road began to dip down a long stretch of hill like the one you see in all the car chase scenes in movies made in San Francisco. I just about shit myself when I saw that, I jumped back on my seat and buckled up, then pointed my index finger at the downward hill.

"Hang on tight," said Eric as the twin turbo engine

kicked in.

"Oh, my God," I said.

The Nissan got to the edge of the hill and flew into the air. I let out a high-pitched scream, as the car was landing. I prayed that we would get out of this alive, and not be arrested for reckless driving. God must have been listening to me because the car landed at the end of the hill just missing a car parked on the side of the street. I glanced in the rearview mirror and noticed the Cadillac was behind us.

"Lily, I have an idea. Just keep down for one more minute," said Eric.

I reluctantly obeyed. I could feel Eric speeding up ever so slightly then without warning the car came to an abrupt stop.

"You can get up now Lily," said Eric.

He handed me a walkie-talkie, the sunglass case and the pocket lie detector.

"Here's what I want you to do. Get out and start walking back in the direction we just came from. I'll explain the rest on the walkie," said Eric.

I got out of the car, putting the items he handed me in my purse. Eric drove off into the distance, as I walked the streets feeling a bit confused as to exactly what I was supposed to be doing. I noticed Frank's car drive by me as I continued walking. I heard a fuzzy noise coming from my purse, so I unzipped it and took out the walkie-talkie.

"Did Frank's car just pass you?" asked Eric.

"Yeah it did. Can you explain to me now what exactly I'm doing out here?" I asked.

"Certainly, see Lily, I wasn't entirely honest with you," said Eric.

"Story of my life," I said aloud, making sure the button on the walkie wasn't pressed down.

"I've been following Frank for about a month, not a week, and lately I've been getting the feeling he was on to me," said Eric.

"I had you duck down so Frank wouldn't see you. I'm hoping Frank spots you, pulls over, and makes a pass at you," said Eric.

"Come on. Do you believe Frank would do something like that? Guys drive by girls all the time without stopping," I replied.

"The way you look Lily, I have a hunch this guy will prove your theory wrong," said Eric.

As flattered as I was to hear this from Eric it made me feel like an undercover whore.

"So, I'm the bait is that it," I said.

"Yes. Now listen. I want you to put on those sunglasses," said Eric.

"Oh, now you want me to put on the sunglasses. Well isn't that convenient. When we were in that surveillance shop, both you and Walter acted as if I wasn't even there. I'm not the type of woman that is to be seen and not heard, I'm a human being, and I expect to be treated that way," I said.

"We can discuss this later, just put on the sunglasses for me, please," said Eric.

I remembered my mission was to catch this guy cheating, so I let the argument go, for now, and put on the glasses. Once I put them on I became disorientated. The sunglasses allow anyone wearing them to look straight ahead, plus see behind you at the same time. There are special coated mirrors on the inside of the wire rim; it gives you the same effect of having eyes in the back of your head.

"Okay I got them on," I said into the walkie.

"Good. Here's what I want you to do. Walk along the streets, and keep an eye out for Frank. Stay in the same area, if Frank doesn't surface after thirty minutes contact me on the walkie," said Eric.

"Wouldn't it be easier and less obvious if I just

called you on your cell phone?" I said.

"Cutting radio silence now," said Eric.

What a weirdo, I thought. Then I switched off the walkie-talkie and put it in my purse.

Walking down the street while having a view of what was behind me took some getting used to. These sunglasses were the metaphor of my life; I was always looking back, wondering if I should've done anything different, I was never able to see clearly what lied ahead. My past had left me with a head full of bad memories, broken hearts, short-lived friendships, and an overall sense of wanting more out of life. Every move I took to achieve my goals seemed to bring me so close, then immediately lead me directly into a huge obstacle that would cause it to fall so far away it was like they were forever out of my reach, and I would be right back where I started. I thought to myself as I stared into the shop windows of downtown Vancouver will I ever be successful? Will I ever find that special someone, that special place where I finally feel awe this is where I belong, that's why all that crap happened. Will I find my happy ending?

As my mind came back to reality, I couldn't help but notice through the mirrored lens someone was staring at my ass. Instinctively I turned around and was face to face with Frank Parker.

"Strange day to be wearing sunglasses don't you think?" Frank asked.

I took the sunglasses off and stared into his eyes. He had a boyish charm about him and I could see why most women would fall for Frank. Then I remembered this guy had a wife, which made my instant attraction become repulsion. Play it cool is what I kept telling myself.

"There's never a bad day to wear sunglasses. I have a bit of a headache so I called in sick, and was on my way to get a coffee. My Doc says caffeine can help get rid of a headache sometimes, and if that doesn't work try sex, he's a bit unorthodox," I said laughing.

"Now I get it. You're undercover, because you're worried that someone might see you from work when you are supposed to be in bed, may I join you for a coffee?" asked Frank.

"Sorry I apologize I should've introduced myself first, my name is Frank," he said.

"Li, I'm, I mean my name is LisBeth, but you can call me Beth, and ya sure you can join me," I replied.

I almost screwed that up, and gave him my real name, I was unprepared for that comment about me being undercover. I had to get my head in the game.

"Tell you what Beth. I know this place just around the corner that makes the best cappuccinos in town. Why don't we go there, my treat?"

"Sounds great," I said as ditzy as possible. You think you are a player Mr., well you've met your match, and the queen is about to make her last move, check mate mother fucker. I knew exactly what I was going to do with Frank to prove he was up to no good, and Frank was falling right into my trap.

Inside the coffee shop the interior design was very urban chic, the menu was listed on chalkboard signs above the cash counter, the color scheme was various shades of brown, with Moroccan styled ceiling lamps and a few arm chairs mixed together with small round wooden tables. I sat down at a two-seater booth as Frank stood in line ordering our coffee. I looked over at Frank while he was checking me out and gave him a fake smile. I urgently needed to get into my purse to pull out the pocket lie detector but his eyes were constantly on me. I carefully unzipped my purse to take out my makeup compact and pretend I was just applying my lip gloss. He kept looking over, I decided to play it safe, I put my gloss on then quickly put my makeup back in my purse leaving it unzipped, since Frank was heading back over to our table.

"One vanilla latte for the lovely lady," said Frank.

I gave Frank a quick wink as I took my first sip. I love a good tasting coffee bean, with perfectly foamed milk. I didn't need drugs to keep me happy, just hand me a well-made latte and I'm in ecstasy. Judging by the flower design created in the milky foam I could tell this barista knew exactly what they were doing. The creamy frothed milk mixed with espresso and vanilla flavoring, all blending inside my mouth was an erotic pleasure, I savored it, it was almost as good as sex.

"You like the flower design? I asked the barista to make it just for you," said Frank.

"Aww, that's so sweet," I said, secretly wanting to gag.

Then came a barrage of questioning. Asking me the typical questions that bore me to death, how old was I, where was I from, what did I do for a living, why did I move there, did I have any kids. All my answers were made up of course. All the while pretending I was hanging off his every word, and making him feel like I was totally into him. As Frank continued to talk I carefully slid my hand inside my purse searching for the pocket lie detector while my eyes rested solely on Frank's. I used the loud background noise from the espresso machine to cover up the sound of my hand ruffling through my purse. Finally, I found the pocket lie detector and switched it on under the table, praying to God I didn't bring attention to what I was doing and make him look under the table out of curiosity. My heart was pounding out of my chest. Now it was my turn to fire off a bunch of questions at Frank.

"So, Frank, tell me a bit about yourself. Like what do you do for a living?" I asked.

"I'm a doctor," said Frank.

I quickly looked down on the pocket lie detector, which indicated he was telling the truth.

"Do you like being a doctor?" I asked.

"Of course, it can be very rewarding at times," said Frank.

The lie detector confirmed this statement was also true.

"Have you ever been married?" I asked.

"Good God no, I haven't found that special someone yet but I'm hoping I will very soon Beth," said Frank.

I looked down at the lie detector and he was telling the truth. Something was wrong. Either the machine was bogus or Frank was such a gifted liar that he could outsmart a lie detector. What if I had the wrong person? I only managed to get a quick glimpse of him in the photo Eric showed me. What were the chances I'd run into a guy with the same first name as his, this had to be him? I had read somewhere that lie detectors are based on emotional responses to the brain. There had to be a way to get Frank out of his head. I needed his responses to be more emotional, and less calculated.

I decided to shock him with this, "I caught the last guy I was with dressing up in my lingerie, he ruined a bunch of my underwear, then he asked me if I would wear a strap on, and fuck him up the ass. Do you think that's normal? Do patients come into your office and talk about their weird sexual desires? Have you ever put on women's clothing?"

Frank gulped down a huge sip of his coffee, practically burning his mouth off, before answering.

"Who me, no never, patients don't usually come to me about their sexual fantasies, and I'm not sure if dressing up in women's clothing is normal, I didn't specialize in psychotherapy," said Frank.

The lie detector suggested there was an eighty percent chance he was lying; I was onto something.

"How about you, do you have a dark side, any weird fantasies?" I said.

"Ah me no, I'm just a regular guy," said Frank.

The meter was registering a seventy percent lie. I was getting warmer.

"What's your favorite position?" I asked.

"I guess I'd have to say the good old-fashioned missionary position," Frank replied.

This time the meter dropped down to a twenty percent chance that he was telling the truth. Time to hit him with an important question again, "And you're sure you aren't married?"

"No not at all," said Frank.

The meter read this as a one hundred percent lie.

"Are you seeing anyone right now?" I asked.

"Nope, free as a bird," said Frank.

Again, another home run for me. My job was done; it was time to escape. I had to get out of there fast.

"That's good Frank. I can tell you're a very honest person," I said finishing the last drop of my latte.

I slid the lie detector back in my purse and shut it off then looked at my watch.

"Well will you look at the time? I got to go," I said standing up.

"Where are you going? Can I get your number?" asked Frank.

"I'm sorry but my phone isn't connected yet," I replied. "Wait a second," said Frank.

He reached into his pocket and handed me a hotel room key.

"Here, take this. I have a room at the Comfort Inn, room #222. I have a business meeting this afternoon but I should be back around six, I'd love it if you were there when I returned. Maybe we can practice some new positions to expand your horizons if you know what I mean," said Frank.

No, I don't know what you mean, and I don't want to know. Men can be so gross sometimes.

"I'll think about it. Got to go. Bye," I said walking out the door.

*** ***

A few blocks later, I contacted Eric on the walkie-talkie, within minutes he picked me up and I told him everything that happened.

"We got him, right?" I asked.

"Not exactly, we still need more proof," said Eric

"Isn't the pocket lie detector enough evidence?" I

said.

"Sadly no, your detective work was commendable yes, but we need more solid proof. Right now, it's your word against his about anything that was said during your meeting," said Eric.

"Well what do you suggest then Eric? I should just waltz right into his hotel room and say hi," I said sarcastically.

Eric was silent.

"Oh no, no, no, I'm not going to do your dirty work for you," I said with disgust.

Eric looked at his watch and back on the road.

"It's one o'clock. The Comfort Inn is only five minutes away from here. That gives you over two hours to search the room. Plenty of time," said Eric.

"Then why can't you do it?" I asked.

"Can't, if I got caught I would lose my P.I. license. Now you on the other hand, since Frank handed you his hotel room key, and invited you back to his room, I don't foresee anything they could charge you with if you got caught in there," said Eric.

"Okay fine, I'll do it," I said.

As Eric drove on, I kept telling myself I was doing the right thing by trying to help another woman discover the truth about her lover. I wished I'd had someone help me catch Arthur before I wasted three years believing his lies. That relationship caused me a lot of heartache. I took a deep breath and kept telling myself in my head, it was meant to be, I was put in this situation for a reason, so I wouldn't lose my nerve.

CHAPTER TWELVE
Wrong Side of the Bed

Inside the hotel lobby, I immediately understood why it was called the Comfort Inn. The furniture and overall vibe felt comfortable; not ugly, not glamorous, simply comfortable. The camera along with the spy gadgets, Eric gave me earlier, weighed a ton. I was paranoid that my purse was going to burst open revealing my intentions for being in this establishment. I walked down the hall as discreetly as possible, grasping my purse with both hands.

Once inside the elevator, I pushed the number two button and went up to the second floor. Before stepping out into the hallway, I looked both ways for any pedestrian traffic, which there was none. Satisfied that I had not been seen I took out the hotel room key and continued down the long corridor. Then my nervous adrenaline kicked in, suddenly I had tunnel vision, it felt like my blood was pulsing intensely through my veins. The pattern on the wallpaper started to swirl, heightening my disorientation. I looked up and saw a glowing exit sign. As much as I wanted to turn back, a voice inside my head kept telling me to persevere. Focus Lily. You can do this. Prove the world wrong, that you are not a loser. You can get through this tunnel of darkness. Look for the light Lily. My eyes landed on the burgundy-carpeted floor focusing on the white diamond design embroidered into the rug, they were like arrows directing where to go. Without warning a shadowy figure emerged from the opposite end of the corridor, it was coming toward me. The closer it came the less I could make it out. Don't pass out Lily. I kept slithering down the hallway almost having to grasp the walls to keep from falling, I didn't want to end up crawling the rest of the way on my hands and knees. Then the stabbing muscle pain hit me like a knife cutting into my skin. Where did this hallway end? It seemed to go on forever. My head felt like it wasn't attached to my body anymore. The shadowy figure was getting closer. That's it Lily, you're almost there. I looked over at the doors trying to make out which number I was at but everything was a blur, nothing was clear. When I looked ahead the shadowy figured was directly above me. Why was I on the floor? I wondered if this was a dream. Had I passed out? Focus Lily. As I pulled myself up trying to make sense of it all the shadow morphed into myself, when I reached out to touch it, it just vanished. The light returned, and my eyesight was clear again. I could see that the door in front of me was number 222, Frank Parker's room. All my senses returned to normal, did I just have a stroke? I had no idea what just happened or any time to waste thinking about it. I was on a mission, and I had to get in and get out. Mental note, see a medical doctor ASAP., and find out what the fuck that was about.

    Looking both left and right, I was relieved to see the hallway was still deserted. I unzipped my purse and pulled out an eyepiece, otherwise known as a reverse peephole viewer. I placed the lens up to the peephole and looked through; to make sure no one was in the room. Did I feel like a Peeping Tom? Yes, but I had a job to do. The room looked dark and empty. I swiped the key and went inside.

    The curtains were drawn letting in very little light. My instincts told me to flip the light switch on but then I realized I didn't want to leave any fingerprints. Despite Eric's reassurance that I wasn't committing a crime, I didn't want to leave behind any evidence that would allow them to identify me, and charge me with trespassing. Taking out a tissue paper, I opened the closet door, only to find it empty. I looked at the time. It was nearly two thirty, there was plenty of time before Frank would return. I walked over to the bed and noticed a small white envelope that was sealed. Curious as to what was inside I held it up to the light but couldn't make anything out. I reached inside my purse and took out a can of aerosol hairspray, I saw this on one of those detective shows. I sprayed the envelope and the paper turned translucent allowing me to see the contents inside. It appeared to be plane tickets to Mexico for two. I quickly grabbed a shot of the envelope with Eric's camera before the envelope returned to its original state. Suddenly I heard voices outside the door. Looking around the room, the only places to hide were either the washroom or the closet. I settled on the closest and shut the door leaving a small crack so I could see what was going on inside the room. The door opened, Frank and a young brown-haired woman with high heels and a short skintight electric blue dress on entered the room embracing each other. This was quite the business meeting Frank had.

"Oh baby. I've been thinking about you all day," said Frank.

Within minutes their clothes were off, followed by

loud moaning. I heard the noise of two bodies slamming onto the king size bed. Hearing these two have sex brought back flashbacks of catching Arthur in bed with that other woman. I felt like crying but held back the tears, that was all the confirmation I needed to know this was where I was supposed to be, and this is what I was meant to be doing. I silently opened the closet door. The two of them were so into it they didn't even notice I was in the room. I had two options; worry about myself and make a quick exit, or expose myself by taking photos to help someone out, then run as fast as I could and hope I made it out safely. I chose the latter. Pulling out the camera I took multiple photos of the two of them in bed naked doing it.

Then I bolted for the door. I could hear Frank calling after me, "Beth. What are you doing here?"

Then I heard his mistress say, "You know her?"

I yelled back just before I entered the stairwell, "You're busted, and my name's not really Beth asshole."

It felt awesome to know I made a difference in someone's life; I finally accomplished something that would help someone else. I ran down the three flights of stairs, once I hit the ground floor I pulled out my walkie and called for Eric to pick me up.

I threw the hotel key at the front desk clerk, and

said, "I won't be needing this," then walked out the front door.

*** ***

As soon as we got back to Eric's place, he decided to have a nap. At first, I thought he was joking but then he proceeded to give me a lecture on how important napping was, informing me that our bodies run on a circadian rhythm.

Again, I wasn't a child and I wasn't interested in having a nap or being schooled by this man. When I told him I wouldn't be joining, he had a hissy fit and stormed off to the bedroom after making sure the entire apartment was in darkness, by closing all the blinds. He asked me not to turn on any lights, the TV, or make any noise for the next three hours.

This was the last straw.

I couldn't take it anymore. I tried my best to see the good in him, tried to find an agent in Vancouver, tried to find a decent serving job, but nothing had panned out. Despite what everyone liked to say about me and how one achieves success, I did try. It never mattered how hard I tried, or how many diplomas I had, it was always my fault I wasn't married, and my fault I wasn't successful. I completely disagree. My anxiety was growing by the day as the remainder of what was in my bank account had shrunk to almost nothing. I knew it was time to move on.

Once Eric fell asleep, I grabbed a piece of paper and wrote him a note.

Dear Eric,

By the time you read this note, I will be gone. There are many reasons as to why I am leaving. Sometimes we are lucky enough to get a sign that we are on the wrong path. Vancouver is not the place for me. I'm homesick, broke, and my acting career isn't taking off. You were a great person for helping me out without even knowing me. Despite how thrilled I was about our success today with the case, I'm just not cut out to be around someone who spies on people. The song 'Private Investigations' by Dire Straits describes exactly how I feel. I have left it on your record player if you care to listen. I appreciate all your hospitality and hope you find someone special.

Sincerely,

Lily Monroe

    I walked over to the fridge, pulled out a lemon, cut it in half, placed it on the table, jabbed a fork in it, and left it beside the letter.

    I walked out the door with my bags in my arms, silently closing it behind me. It's ironic the album was titled *Love Over Gold*. I knew if I stuck it out with Eric, I'd have a good life, but like the album title said, I prefer love over gold.

    As I drove off, I imagined Eric reading the note with the song playing in the background.

CHAPTER THIRTEEN
The Long Way Home

I should've checked the weather before I left. I was stupid. I wasn't thinking. All that was on my mind was the desire to be home. It's one thing to drive up north during a snowstorm. It's another story driving through the Rocky Mountains during an ice storm.

It was my first night of driving, and my first time navigating through the Rocky Mountains. I wanted to drive as far as I could, and get as close to home as I could. It was around midnight when I hit black ice on that mountain road; my car sped up and started to fishtail. I couldn't steer out of it because I had no road to steer out of it with. This was a narrow two-lane highway that wound through a steep mountain range. I panicked and touched the brakes to try to slow down. I know that is exactly what I wasn't supposed to do, but I couldn't maneuver my car on that road at the speed I was traveling. I had to touch my brakes. After that I started to do 360's and lost complete control, there was nothing I could do. My car was spinning in circles, out of control. I closed my eyes slammed on the brakes and prayed. The first moment of impact was when the passenger side slammed into the mountain, then my car spun around and the back bumper hit the mountain. There I was stuck in the side of a mountain, my car had stalled, and there was a transport truck headed in my direction. I was a nervous wreck, I wasn't ready to drive, I was thinking I would just calm down and stay there for a bit. I'd just had a near death experience. I wasn't even sure my heart had started beating again. I also wasn't sure if the transport could even see me. My silver Audi could've been completely camouflaged by the winter snow. The transport truck was getting closer by the second. I had to see if my car would start and pull out before I got crushed. Just in the nick of time the engine started, I pulled out of the mountain and drove to the first hotel I could find.

When I parked the car, I immediately jumped out to assess the damage. I was afraid to look at first, then much to my surprise I only found two issues, one I couldn't open the passenger side door, and two there were some indentations on the rear bumper. I was shocked and grateful that my car was not only in one piece but barely even scathed by such a traumatic incident. I could've plunged off a cliff and either died on impact, or been stuck there for days until I died from injuries, or hypothermia. I was one lucky girl, and believed in God from that moment on. I downed two shots of vodka from the mini bar to calm my nerves, and then went to sleep. I still had a long ride ahead of me before I reached home.

    The next day as I continued through the mountain range in daylight I realized just how close to death I had come. Perhaps last night's incident was a wakeup call from God. I felt energized; I had a new lease on life. I had to have been put on this earth for a reason. It was time to go after my dreams with a vengeance. It was time to find a real man, I had to become a force to be reckoned with when it came to finding love. No more wearing my heart on my sleeve, or settling for the wrong guy. During this revelation, my thoughts were quickly turned back to the road ahead once I realized driving in the daytime was not going to be a breeze compared to driving at night. I was wrong, whether I was climbing the mountain, or descending, both were so steep and the road was so narrow, I had white knuckles as I grasped my steering wheel in fear of flying off the ridge the entire time. It was terrifying.

*** ***

By dinnertime, I had finally made it through the Rocky Mountains and reached the city of Calgary. I could breathe a sigh of relief I thought, nope wrong again. The ice storm had blown through the entire city, leaving all the streets, including the highway, covered by a sheet of ice. I almost rear ended a car just trying to stop on a merge ramp to get back on the highway. Fuck this, as much as I wanted to stop and rest there for the night, there was no way I was driving around a city of ice to look for accommodations.

I high tailed it out of there as fast as I could. I'd had enough close calls for one trip. I chugged vanilla lattes by the dozen from every gas station I stopped at, stretched my legs, splashed water on my face in the bathroom, and then got right back on the road. I drove for twenty-four hours straight that day, until I was shaking so badly from fatigue or caffeine that I couldn't drive anymore. I prayed my credit card would be able to fit a cheap hotel on it, and stopped for the night in Thunder Bay, Ontario. I needed to shower, and sleep.

A phone call from the front desk woke me up in the middle of the night, and scared the shit out of me. They were calling to inform me that my credit card had been declined. I had to get up, get dressed and go down there. I was able to squeeze twenty dollars on my card, then used the cash I had in my wallet to cover the rest, that was my money for food and gas to get me the rest of the way home. It was still a fourteen-hour drive away. I could feel the tension in my body from all the stress. I swear, I could've have slept another week there if I could afford to.

    In the morning, I found a bank machine, withdrew my last forty dollars, filled up the tank, armed myself with an extra-large vanilla latte then set out to make it home that night.

    Ignoring the speed limit signs, I put the car into over drive, since there were no mountains to contend with. All I could see for miles and miles were clear roads and straightaways, perfect. I was going over one hundred miles per hour, making great time I'd be home by ten p.m., until I looked up and realized there was a highway patrol car in my rearview mirror. I had no idea how long he'd been there or if he was following me. I'd been doing at least sixty over the speed limit for over an hour. I couldn't afford a speeding ticket, or the damage that would do to my insurance. Oh, my God, I just couldn't catch a break. I just wanted to see my family again, and get home before I ran out of money. I thought about flooring it, and trying to outrun the cop, maybe there was a side street I could duck out on. What was I a fugitive, sometimes I wonder about the thoughts that go through my mind? Just then, he switched on his lights and siren. Maybe he was in pursuit of a criminal, and that wasn't for me. I got into the right lane so he could pass me, but he followed behind, it was me he was after. The fatigue of driving for days without much sleep was clouding my judgment. I pulled off to the side of the road; the highway patrol officer got out of his vehicle and started walking toward me. He was a short fat bald man that looked to be in his late forties. He was looking at the back of my car, he must've noticed the damage from the accident in the mountains, then he came to the side signaling me to roll down my window. I didn't want to; it was freezing outside. I put on my gloves to make sure I didn't get frostbite before obliging the officers request. I fucking hate getting pulled over. I always act like an idiot because it makes me so angry, which guarantees the cop gives me a ticket. Note to self, learn to control my raging anger toward cops who pull me over, especially if I'm guilty. When I finished rolling down the window, I could sense this guy was undressing me with his eyes, it was disgusting, he was a total pervert.

"Good day, Miss. Going somewhere in a hurry?" asked the officer.

I sat there like an idiot and didn't respond.

"Did you not see me following you for the last twenty minutes?" he said. I sat there in silence.

"If you don't answer me I'm going to have to ask you to get out of the vehicle, and come down to the station with me," he replied.

"No, I didn't see you," I said.

"You could've killed someone at the speed you were going," he said.

I still sat there looking stupid. There wasn't anything I could say or do to fix this, I was terrible at talking my way out of tickets. I was speeding for my own good, so I could get home safe and off the road before I fell asleep at the wheel.

"Well aren't you going to say anything?" he asked.

Then, as if right on cue, the tears began to flow.

"I'm sorry. I'm a mess. I've been driving for days without any sleep. All I want to do is get home," I said. The officer rolled his eyes.

"I've heard it all before young lady. Where did that damage on the back come from? Was this car in an accident recently?" he asked.

"No, I was driving through the Rocky Mountains and hit a patch of black ice. My car spun out of control, I narrowly missed flying off a cliff, by slamming my car into the side of the mountain," I said.

"That sounds like a bunch of bullshit to me," he said.

"It's the truth, I swear," I said.

"License and registration please," said the officer.

"You have got to be kidding. I don't have a penny to my name, my credit card is maxed out, can you let me go please I'm begging you. Can't you please just let me go, I promise I will drive carefully, and stop speeding. What can I do to convince you to let me off the hook?" I said. The way the officer licked his lips sent shivers up my spine.

"There is something you can do for me, if you step out of the car and take a walk with me over to my vehicle I'll show you in the back," he said.

I couldn't believe my ears. I've heard horror stories of women being taken advantage of by corrupt cops but I never thought it would happen to me.

"Does this favor involve getting a lift or being taken for a ride?" I asked.

"You could say that missy. I think we both know what I'm getting at," said the officer.

"Really, I'm glad we cleared that up. See that cell phone over there?" I said pointing to my dashboard.

"What about it?" he asked.

"My phone is voice activated and just recorded everything you said."

"You're bluffing," he said.

"Am I? We can always take this up in court, I'm sure your boss, and the judge would love to hear what you just said to me. Shall I play it back for you?" I asked.

"No Ma'am, that won't be necessary," he said.

"Can I go now?"

"Yes Ma'am, you can go, just slow down on the roads and drive safe, okay," the officer advised.

"Sounds fair and don't call me ma'am," I playfully ordered while waving goodbye with a huge grin on my face.

Once the highway patrol car was out of sight, I tried to check the time on my cell phone. Crap. The phone was dead. I plugged it into the lighter to charge it while I went on my way. I couldn't wait to get home.

The rest of the trip I played it safe by driving the speed limit. When I finally reached the *Welcome to Toronto* sign, I breathed a sigh of relief. Holy shit, I was finally home and in one piece.

When I walked through the door of my parents' condominium, located right across from Square One, Mississauga's major shopping center, I arrived to a very blasé welcome. It was disappointing. I felt different too. I wasn't the same Lily that had left there a few months ago. This was a stronger, wiser, improved version, whom had learned from her past. My mom got up and went straight to her room, that hurt. I thought she'd be happy to see me. I was in no mood to be lectured so I went directly to my old room and passed out from sheer exhaustion, looking forward to waking up to a brighter future.

Chapter Fourteen
A New Beginning

The year is nineteen ninety-seven.

My parents agreed to let me move back in with them until I could pay off my debt. The first thing I did was call my agent and ask if she would take me back, to my delight, she said yes. The next thing I did was apply for a job at the SkyDome.

The third thing I did was make an appointment to see our family physician and tell him about the episode I had in Vancouver in the hallway at the Comfort Inn. I hadn't felt normal since that day. Everyone kept telling me that it was stress, but I could barely function.

Everyone else was working full time, looking after

a family, working out. I could barely get out of bed. Then I thought it was the long drive home, but when it continued after I got back home, I was concerned. I was tired all the time, my body was killing me, I was getting severe headaches, I was in pain everywhere, all the time. I felt like I was ninety years old. My Doctor did a physical exam, touching several points on my body, then said I had a condition called Fibromyalgia. Then, he asked if I had been in an accident as an infant and suffered severe head trauma. I couldn't remember my parents saying I had been in any accidents. He said that I must've had some type of childhood injury, and that combined with the stress of moving out west had activated this autoimmune disease.

    I was only thirty years old. I had considerable debt. After reading, only a few articles I found out that I had something that makes most of its victims bedridden. Some people even commit suicide after years of having this illness. I was lucky I lived with my parents, but I still had to support myself. I had to pay off school loans, pay for my car. I got my old job back and started waitressing again. I couldn't work more than fifteen hours a week, that didn't cover any of my bills. I applied for disability but was turned down. I didn't know how to fight the system. I'd never fought any battles in my life. It was too difficult for me to figure out how to fight the government, when I was struggling just to put two feet on the ground and haul myself out of bed every morning. I didn't look sick, which made my life even more challenging. I would try to explain it to people that were wondering why I didn't work more, they just looked at me in disbelief and treated me horribly after. I realized it would be better for me to hide how sick I felt as best I could. Being bullied because I wasn't well, was something I didn't need to be dealing with. My health was deteriorating rapidly. My doctor's only advice was to exercise, and try swimming. Both of which made it even worse. I didn't know where to turn. My own parents didn't even believe I was sick. My guilt made this whole ordeal even more difficult. My parents were in their sixties I was supposed to be helping them retire not have them help me. I was so disappointed where my life was.

I started reading every and anything I could find written about this condition. I had to become my own doctor. This could not be how I lived out the rest of my life. I ended up learning a lot about the human body, food, digestion, I got to know my body very well, what I could, and couldn't do. There was a fine balance between work, and rest, that I had to adhere to or I would suffer months and months of even worse physical setbacks. How I was going to juggle work, auditioning, and working out with this condition was something else that weighed heavy on my mind.

In my humble opinion, a clear majority of doctors will easily prescribe drugs that treat symptoms but they are by no means interested in finding a cure. For me, drugs to mask the symptoms were not an option. The side effects ended up being worse than the illness itself.

It's a problem that most doctors are closed minded, they don't realize how much they could've helped me by sending me to a naturopath. I understand it goes against everything they spent years learning in med school but the truth is the only medical professionals that helped get me back on my feet, were practitioners that believed in other sciences. I needed integrative medicine, it took a team of chiropractors, naturopaths, and physiotherapists that were open to the understanding they did not singularly have the cure for me to help me. I thought people became doctors to help sick people get better, it didn't make sense to me that they were completely shut off to the idea of alternative medicine. Some doctors don't even believe fibromyalgia exists. My response was I don't care what you call it, these are my symptoms, write them down and tell me how to get rid of them. Call it whatever you want, don't call it anything, but help me get better. They didn't like that much. I was starting to think I was smarter than they were. I stopped seeing M.D.'s.

I finally got a call for an interview at the SkyDome, I wasn't sure if I could work there due to this health issue I was dealing with, but a girl I went to Ryerson with told me the servers there made a fortune during baseball season, maybe this would be a blessing in disguise. I filled out the application while I waited for the manager to join me at the table. I was in the restaurant J10 that overlooked the baseball field where the Toronto Blue Jays played, and our new N.B.A. team called the Raptors. After a few questions, he sent over the general manager for a second interview, by the end of the day I got the call that I was hired.

The décor and food was simple, nothing fancy. Nachos, burgers, chicken wings were the staples on the menu. The tablecloths were quite gaudy, and made of cheap plastic with a blue and white-checkered pattern, like something you'd see on a picnic table. Along the walls and ceiling hung various sports memorabilia, as well as photos of famous baseball players, signed by them and framed. The bar was made of a dark wood, possibly pine, it was cut in the shape of a baseball bat.

Most visitors knew exactly what this establishment

was, a tourist trap with cool souvenirs, a great atmosphere, beer, and fast food. The best part was that you could watch a live game while you enjoyed a meal and an alcoholic beverage.

I had been at the J10 a few months when I heard all the girls squealing, they were in a frenzy about someone who was dining in the restaurant. The night before one of the servers managed to get the attention of one of the Blue Jay players from the field during the game and now he was in the restaurant having lunch. At the time, I wasn't into watching sports. There were a few famous names I knew due to the level of success they had reached; but overall, I had no clue who any of the professional baseball players were.

The restaurant was practically empty when I arrived in my street clothes wearing a pair of white track pants, a white cropped sweater and wedge sneakers. I walked over to the section he was sitting in and poked my head around the corner to check out what all the fuss was about. He looked right at me, I was embarrassed, instantly backed up, and ran out to the change room to put my J10 uniform dress on.

Inside the change room, I thought to myself this was not love at first sight, but there was a definite attraction.

When I went back inside I noticed his golden skin it went nice with his twinkling white teeth that accentuated his deep brown eyes and luscious full lips. He had a nice toned, fit physique, which could be seen underneath his light knit Armani sweater, and dark fitted jeans. The knit was just light enough to show off his six-pack. He was flashy, and made it obvious he made a lot of money, by wearing a diamond encrusted Rolex watch, a diamond necklace with a diamond cross, and expensive designer clothing. Still the visual wasn't enough, I didn't feel like I was dying to go out with this guy, that was of course until I heard him speak. Anyway, one of my coworkers was the reason for him being there I had to put him in the back of my mind. I didn't want to interfere with the other girl.

    While I was in my section checking the condiments to make sure they were full, I could feel him staring at me. I turned around to look and there he was, turned around in his chair staring right at me. I kept my cool and walked over to the upper level to polish cutlery, as he sat and continued to eat below. He looked up at me, got out of his chair, then walked up to the railing below me, and said in a thick Spanish accent, "My name is Alejandro, but you can call me Alex. I was wondering if you would like to go out some time?"

I felt like I was in the balcony scene from Romeo & Juliet. He didn't waste much time he was straight forward, when this man sees something he likes he goes for it. I admired that, plus he asked me out with the most romantic accent I'd ever heard.

"That would be nice," I replied.

"What is your phone number?" he asked.

I looked around the restaurant cautiously. I didn't want any of my coworkers to see what was happening. I didn't know what the policy was in terms of going out with any of the baseball players.

"I can't write it down," I whispered under my breath.

"Say it out loud, I'll memorize it," said Alex.

After I said each number quietly, he repeated it in Spanish, again with the most romantic sounding accent I'd ever heard, I was mesmerized.

I'd been single for just over a year now, and could count the amount of dates I'd had on one hand. Yet, there was this nagging feeling that my coworker was the one who signaled him to come up there. Then he makes a move on me not her, what is a girl to do? Was it wrong to go out with him? I decided that I would never tell her or anyone else that we worked with that he asked for my number.

The next day she conveniently ended up quitting her job with us, to go back to working full time in an office. But then I also didn't hear a thing from Alex which seemed odd since he was so aggressive at approaching me. As I was working my shift, I couldn't help but notice the Jays were on the field warming up before the game. I looked across the field for Alex and when our eyes met, he signaled me to come over. I managed to make up an excuse to take a five-minute break and ran down to meet him in the stands.

"Why haven't you called me?" asked Alex.

"What are you talking about?" I asked.

"Go check your messages," he said. I ran back to the change room, and pulled out my cell phone. Yes, I had to go get it from my locker, imagine that. Back then we didn't walk around with our phones attached to our hands full time. How could I have forgotten to check my messages? Of course, I forgot, I had fibromyalgia brain; I kept forgetting that I had that, or perhaps I should say I kept trying to forget that I had an incurable, debilitating illness, I couldn't remember the slightest thing anymore. It was annoying, like having Alzheimer's, the flu, and a hangover at the same time, all while trying to pretend I felt perfectly fine. He had called me yesterday just before the game and left a message for me to call him back. Without hesitation, I called him right after I heard the message and we agreed to meet after the game in one of the other restaurants in the SkyDome. I begged my manager to cut me early, raced home as fast as I could, and jumped in the shower. As I was showering, I could hear my cell phone ring. Running naked out of the shower, almost wiping out on the wet floor, I grabbed the phone just in time, it was Alex checking to make sure I was still coming, which I said yes to and continued frantically getting ready before he changed his mind.

I rushed to the mall, bought a new outfit, ran home changed into it, broke my perfume bottle trying to put perfume on in the elevator because I was rushing around like a maniac desperate for a date. Damn it, smarten up Lily this date is not the end of the world, and it's costing you a fortune.

When I got there Alex was sitting at the bar, looking even more gorgeous than he did the first day I saw him. He was such a gentleman, warm, friendly and treated me like a lady. I was nervous and a bit intimidated by his money and success. I didn't know why, but I was. My insecurity about not having a successful career myself got the better of me that night. I knew very little about baseball so I wasn't sure what to talk about either. Luckily, he didn't seem to notice, and kept the conversation going himself.

"Where are you from?" I asked. There it was that sexy, gorgeous accent when he replied, "Venezuela."

After a few drinks and some small talk, a much older Venezuelan couple in their fifties entered the room.

"Lily, do me a favor, act like we've known each other for years," said Alex.

Not knowing why, I nodded quietly in agreement. He then put his arm around my waist.

"Alejandro, Como Estas?" said the older man in Spanish.

He was tall, well dressed in a charcoal gray suit, white dress shirt and a baby blue tie. His salt and pepper hair gave him a regal look like George Clooney. The woman that hung on his arm lit up the room in her mini emerald green sequin dress. Her pièce de résistance were the sparkling diamonds that surrounded her large emerald earrings. Her long wavy auburn hair flowed beautifully with her glowing skin.

"Lily, I'd like you to meet my manager, Enzo Massiani," said Alex.

Enzo took my hand and kissed it.

"It is a pleasure meeting you Lily. This is my wife,

Sophia."

"Hello Lily, it's a pleasure," said Sophia.

The restaurant we were in was upscale, with a nice lounge and a full dining room, they also had floor-to-ceiling windows that overlooked the field. We were positioned right above center field.

Enzo signaled to the waiter and ordered us a bottle of white wine. I would've rather had Grey Goose and diet Coke but I realized it was only polite to drink what the gentleman ordered.

Alex still had his arm around me and was trying to kiss me on the cheek. I turned my head to say something to him and the kiss that was meant for my cheek ended up on my lips. It was our first kiss. I would remember it forever. His lips were spectacular. He was so affectionate toward me in front of them that it made me feel like we had known each other for years. I felt like we were a real couple. I didn't care that the two of them were staring at us as we kissed but I could tell Sophia wasn't too thrilled. "How long have you two being going out?" asked Sophia.

I looked at Alex, he looked at me; I didn't know what to say. One of us needed to speak, I thought he would take care of their questions, they were his friends. I didn't know what lies I could get away with. I still didn't understand why it mattered.

"A few years," said Alex.

After we ate he grabbed my hand and pulled me out of my seat then started dancing the Bachata with me, he was holding me close, swirling me around the room like a professional dancer, while singing the words in Spanish in my ear as the song played in the background. This was the most romantic gesture I'd ever experienced; I was completely swept away. After the song ended, he asked if I wanted to take the party upstairs to one of the rooms in the SkyDome hotel. I said I wasn't sure. Where was my coach, I needed a first base coach to help get me through this moment, should I head to second base, or go straight home? Then he said we could go back to his place if I preferred. I prefer to be your girlfriend and have a ring on my finger before I make any of these choices if you must know, I thought to myself. I knew that neither choice was a good idea. I should just thank him for the date, and go home but I just didn't have it in me. It had been over a year since I'd been with someone. The thought of all those nights I spent alone, and the thought of leaving him to go home to lie in bed once again alone made it impossible for me to call it a night.

We decided to leave Enzo and Sophia alone and

went to Alex's hotel room. We ended up twenty steps in front of the room service guy that was delivering drinks to our room. Every five steps Alex would stop me in the hall, press me up against the wall, make out with me, until the room service guy caught up then we would take off giggling. When we kissed, I melted into his arms, it felt like he was making love to my mouth. His kisses were an art form full of a variety of sucking, biting, and swirling of the tongue in utter perfection. I loved this date, and this moment in my life. I was also thinking, Lily go home. This is where things could go wrong. Just say thank you for a wonderful night, and go home.

When we got back to the room Enzo and Sophia were seated on the bed drinking champagne. How the hell did they get there, and why were they here? I wondered.

"Would you care for a glass?" asked Enzo.

"No thank you, I'll have vodka and diet Coke please," I said.

As Enzo grabbed the bottle of vodka from the ice bucket, Alex and I stood at the window for a moment, holding hands looking down onto the field. I had looked onto this field countless times from work but for some reason it looked different that night, it looked magical. It became my field of dreams. Dreams I'd never had, but suddenly it was the life I could see myself living. The thought of being up in a room overlooking the baseball field my husband was playing on below was surreal. I saw myself and Alex running the bases playfully after a game laughing, smiling, we looked so happy. Alex seemed like my dream guy, he was warm, friendly, outgoing, passionate. At that moment, I had a feeling my future was going to be bright.

I walked over to one of the chairs and sat down. Alex started doing a strip tease for me, which was somewhat odd since the other couple was still in the room. I didn't want him to feel stupid so I tried to play along. I felt his chest, his skin was smooth and hairless.

I didn't know if they wanted to have some sort of kinky foursome, but I wasn't having any of it. I was not into that type of sexual experience; I wanted Alex all to myself. I looked at Alex then looked at Enzo and Sophia. Alex picked up on this, he said something to Enzo in Spanish who then picked up the hotel phone, and pushed the button to front desk. Enzo and Sophia got up and exited the room.

After they left I was seduced out of the chair and onto the floor. He was performing the most mind-blowing foreplay I'd ever experienced. It started with him gently sucking my boobs out of my bra and then slowly moving down my body as he gently sucked and licked every inch of me until he reached my crotch. Then he sucked my lips out of my underwear. Wow. There was not one part of my body that went unappreciated. It was at that moment that I learned the erotic pleasure that came from someone licking my ass. He licked, and sucked me from my crotch to my ass. All I could think of was that I was not prepared for this, I would've done some extra primping if I'd known someone was going to go to town down there. He had me lying on my back on the floor, then suddenly without any warning he flips me upside down lifting me up off the floor and carried me to the bed with my legs over his shoulder while continuing to eat me out. Then he lowered me onto the bed and continued to lick and suck me dry. I was on a natural high. He was on top then I was on top. He was determined that we were going to climax together. I was thinking we're in for a long night if you're determined to make that happen. I had to fake it, he was not going to give up.

When we finished fooling around we sat up and watched television. Every time I got up to go to the bathroom when I returned he had his arm out waiting for me to snuggle in. I jumped right in there and snuggled. He then wrapped his arms around me and played with my nose. I felt like a giddy school girl. I was so happy. The feeling of fulfillment and contentment washed over me like a dream. It was three a.m. when we fell asleep cuddled up in each other's arms.

When I woke up I kept debating if I should stay or go. My mom knew who I was out with and if I didn't come home, I was afraid she'd know why and be disappointed in me. At the same time, I was worried he would never call me again. Every time I kept trying to leave he would squeeze me in closer, asking me to stay. At five a.m., I said I have to go and took off.

*** ***

When I handed the valet guy the ticket for my car, he asked me how my night went. I thought that was wildly inappropriate and odd but since I was on a natural high and in LaLa Land, I was dying to share the experience I just had with anyone that asked.

I answered by simply saying, "Amazing."

Then got in my car and drove home. I'm guessing the room service staff saw us kissing in the hallway and rumors went around who I was with. At the time, Alex was popular, even though I didn't have a clue who he was, it seemed like everyone else did.

Two days later, Alex invited me over to his condo. We ordered in pizza, watched a movie, cuddled, and had sex. When I was on my way to the bathroom to shower, he pointed to his dresser. Then told me I should be more careful as he lifted a towel revealing a camcorder. I asked if it was turned on, he said, "No, of course not."

I trusted him. After that night, he never returned my calls. Whenever we saw each other I was working and he was on the field practicing. Alex would wave at me from the field in a flirty way, but never called me again. I didn't let it bother me. Out of all the men I dated, up to that point, Alex was the one who created the most memorable sensual experience. Although I wished that night was the beginning of something that lasted forever, at least I had the memory of it. He was the guy who crushed my field of dreams. He was also the guy going to court a year later for videotaping a sexual experience he had with his girlfriend against her will. The *Toronto Sun* informed me of this when they called me for an interview, hoping it was me. They dug me up from the archives of their emails. An email I sent them after I read their story on Alex and his opinion of local women and groupies, compared to his Venezuelan princess'. I had attached a rebuttal article I wanted them to print so readers, for once, could get the female side of the story when it comes to dating professional athletes. They had dismissed it.

Chapter Fifteen
Sweet Spot

  Ever since meeting Alex, I was dying to have an experience like that again. I was afraid that wanting to feel like that again had become an addiction. I also noticed there was a weird atmosphere at work. Some of my coworkers were giving me the cold shoulder. My guess is that someone had overheard my conversation with Alex when he asked me for my number. I was getting a mixed vibe. Half of them seemed angry, competitive, and jealous. The other half wanted to get closer to me suddenly, and started asking me if I wanted to hang out with them,

  Hmm, opposite reactions. I didn't have any close friends at the time so I went along with their game in the hopes they would get to know the real Lily and start liking me for who I am.

Christine was the first one who approached me to go out. She was bubbly, in her early twenties, with stunning blue eyes, and long raven hair. Christine was Kardashian curvy and proud of it. She had a year around tan, courtesy of our local indoor tanning salon, which she eventually got a job at to eliminate the accumulating expense of tanning three times a week.

After work, Christine and I decided to go for a pre-drink at a restaurant called *Muse*, before we hit the club scene.

I discovered *Muse* by accident one day. It was located about a block away from the SkyDome. I was walking back to my car after work one night when a man rushed outside onto the street, telling me that he was the owner of this place and wanted to buy me a drink. I tilted my head up and saw a white and purple sign in cursive font reading, *Muse*. The letter M was larger than the other letters; it swooped down so invitingly, then curved around the rest of the name. I considered the restaurant from the sidewalk and could see that the place was buzzing. I accepted his drink offer out of curiosity. I had to know why people flocked to this establishment. If I were judging it by looks alone, I would never have noticed it. It looked like the average King St. bistro.

Once I was inside the restaurant, sitting down having a glass of white wine, I started to look around, and noticed each wall was covered with framed photos of the owner who had invited me in, posing with countless celebrity athletes from every sport you could think of.

I guess you can't judge a book by its cover, this place was a hot spot for celebrities and I'd never even noticed it before. I can't tell you the names but I can tell you this, these men and women were at the top of their competitive sports, it was the best of the best in those pictures. I never thought of looking for a celebrity hang out, for some reason one had just found me. I didn't know it at the time, but I was about to fall down the rabbit hole and had no clue how to handle myself in the world I landed in on the other side.

After a few drinks, we were still undecided where to go dancing, that's when these two tall guys walked in. The shorter one I recognized as playing for the Blue Jays and the taller one I assumed must have as well. The taller one was more attractive to me, with his flawless complexion, his height being way over six feet tall, along with his muscular body, blue eyes, and dirty blond hair. They walked straight to the back and sat down. I don't think they even noticed us.

"Which one do you like?" asked Christine.

"I don't know if I like either of them," I said.

Just then the bartender interrupted our conversation when she came over to our table to tell us the two men sitting at the table in the back would like to buy us a drink. I looked over to where the bartender was pointing and sure enough, it was the two men that we had just watched enter the restaurant. The taller one waved at me and smiled.

"I'll have a Grey Goose and diet Coke," I said.

"And for you, Miss?" said the bartender.

"A triple of the most expensive vodka you have on the menu mixed with red bull, please," said Christine.

The bartender waved her hand in the air signaling the two guys to come up to the front of the restaurant to join us. They walked over and sat across from us. The taller one was named Nick and the shorter one was Shane.

"Where are you ladies off to tonight?" asked Nick. "We were thinking of checking out a club called Lobby. Want to come with us?" I asked. Without hesitation, we finished our drinks and all four of us piled into my car.

When we got to Lobby, the lineup was insane. Nick talked to the bouncer who allowed him to go inside to check it out. A few seconds later Nick ran back out.

"Forget it. It's too packed. (He probably ran into a bunch of women he had slept with.) Know anywhere else to go?" he asked.

"Yeah. Atelier's busy on Wednesday nights," I said.

"Is it good?" asked Shane.

"Who cares? Let's go," said Nick.

When we got inside Atelier it was busy. There were a couple of other Blue Jay players there. We all hung out in the VIP section. I didn't cling to them while other girls were trying to talk to them, we weren't on a date with them. I also had no idea who was into who, or if anyone was into anyone at all. Then Nick reached out and pulled me toward him by the back of my red halter top, O.k. well now there is a little clue I thought to myself. We weren't there very long when he decided he wanted to leave. He invited us back to his place.

He lived in a huge two-bedroom brand-new condo. When we got inside Christine became very antisocial. She was sitting on a couch by herself not talking to anyone, and had zipped her coat up to the top. I think she was jealous that I got Nick and she wasn't going to settle for Shane just because he was there. I don't know why she couldn't act decent for these two nice, decent, successful guys. I wasn't sure where to sit, because I still wasn't sure if he was that into me. My friend was on one side of the room, his teammate was on the other, and Nick was still in the kitchen. I was the only one who had to make the choice of where to sit. I sat on the edge of the couch that was empty, two minutes later Nick jumped over the back of the couch, sat down, reached out and pulled me on the couch next to him. That put a big smile on my face. Then he reached up pulled a blanket over our heads, wrapped his big strong arms around me, pulled me in close to him, and gave me a soft passionate kiss on the lips. It felt amazing.

His next words were, "If I gave your friend money to take a cab home would you stay?"

I didn't think twice, I said yes.

We went from the living room to his bedroom after everyone left. Then the stupidest shit flew out of my mouth.

"Nick, you're not the first sports player I've been with," I said.

I was nervous and had been drinking. I was afraid he would find out I'd been with Alex.

"Are you trying to get yourself kicked out?" asked Nick.

I couldn't put my thoughts together in my intoxicated stupor to explain why I said that. I wasn't this girl, I shouldn't have been there, I was a girlfriend type of girl. I had to figure a way out of his place before I made another mistake. I was worried this would cause me to end up alone forever. In the meantime, the voice inside my head got shut off when my emotions took over and felt how amazing it was to lie in this gorgeous man's arms. I decided to have faith that something meaningful could come out of this night.

As these thoughts swirled around in my head, and the debate ended, I looked up from the bed and realized Nick was standing half-naked above me, and what a perfect vision that was. There was no turning back at this point. I'd had too much alcohol to drive home or let's be real play the role of the untouched virgin. Every inch of him from head to toe was solid muscle, and defined. All the blood rushed out of my head and there was no more thinking after that. I couldn't wait to keep kissing him and feel what it was like to have him inside me. It was huge, he was passionate, the entire experience was deeply satisfying.

Once we finished and were lying in bed next to each other, he put his arm around me, and cuddled up to me. I felt comfortable, content, happy for the first time in a long time. I also thought I should go look in the mirror, to make sure I don't have makeup smudged all over my face, but I didn't check. I didn't want to move in case this moment disappeared forever.

"Do you have a boyfriend?" asked Nick.

"No, I don't," I replied.

"When was the last time you were in a relationship?" asked Nick.

Thinking back to Eric that didn't count so I told him very briefly about myself and Arthur. Then he started to get even more personal, asking me questions like had I ever been married, did I have any kids and if I normally leave clubs with guys. I'm not sure where this line of questioning came from. Of course, being the girl that I was I chose to think it meant he was interested in me. Unfortunately for me all the honest answers to those questions were embarrassing. I told him that I was single, but not how long I'd been single, my last real relationship had been over three years ago, no kids and no I didn't want any, just what every man wants to hear, it makes me sound so loving and maternal. I'd never been married or proposed to and no, I never leave clubs with guys, that was my only lie. He was probably thinking wow what's wrong with this chick. Then Nick asked me a strange question.

"Lily, are you a player?" I couldn't believe he asked that.

Was the term player his polite way of asking if I

was a slut? Correct me if I'm wrong but it takes two people to have sex. Men and women are no different. We both have the need to feel emotionally connected to another human being. We both need affection, and occasionally to experience physical pleasure when we are lonely, and single. Why he asked these questions after having sex God only knows.

"No, I'm not a player, but thanks for asking," I said with a chuckle.

He was the kind of guy you get that boyfriend feeling from right away, due to his warm, affectionate, playful personality. I didn't doubt for a second that women fell head over heels for this guy. He had that effect on me and I didn't even know him yet. If anything, he was a player, and a damn good one at that.

The next morning at **6:00** A.M., his team was leaving for a road trip. I felt like shit. Hangover, headache, I could barely get dressed. I wasn't even supposed to be drinking it made my condition worse, plus the doctor said that damn fibromyalgia had damaged my liver. Which is why a substantial portion of my income went toward purchasing a liver detoxifying powder that I had to take for the rest of my life. I ran into the bathroom to freshen up, aww I looked in the mirror, and just as I had feared the night before, there was black mascara all under my eye's that made me look like something out of a horror flick. I knew I should've checked. I had to get it together fast, I touched up my makeup as best I could, then out the door I went and straight into the walk of shame through the lobby, which had the bonus of seeing his teammates as I walked out the front door. I pulled my huge fur lined *Dsquared2* bomber hood up over my face, got in my car and headed straight home. This was the second sports player that went after me. I didn't think much of it. I didn't let it go to my head. All I wanted was a long-term meaningful relationship with a man. I wasn't out to land a famous athlete. These one-night stands were fun, but not what I was after. It was a band-aid, a temporary fix to break up months and months of sitting at home alone. What do they call that, a double-edged sword I believe?

    As soon as I got home, I took a handful of painkillers, and went to bed, dreaming of an everlasting love that was mutual, honest and pure. I didn't care what others thought of my dreams, I knew the kind of love that I was looking for existed, it didn't just happen in the movies, it could happen in life. All I had to do was have faith. Oh, and stop drinking, perhaps.

CHAPTER SIXTEEN
Go Big or Go Home

I spent the next two years being "good". I didn't go home with anyone, I didn't have sex, I also didn't go on dates. Not going to clubs and not sleeping with a man didn't change one damn thing. I won't bore you with the details of those two years, to sum it all up, I worked, cycled, shopped, went out for coffee, hung out with my mom, vacationed with my mom, and sat in my room going bat shit crazy from loneliness.

It was the morning after I broke my two years of solitude. I was so hung over.

I shoved my head under my pillow as I heard my mom yelling from the living room that Betsy had been trying to get a hold of me. I was delighted to hear that, at first anyway. She was a friendly face and a true friend that would be comforting right now. Then I remembered her bipolar personality. Maybe we could have a fresh start and things would be different. I picked up my cell phone and called her. She was frantic on the other end of the phone. She asked if I could meet up with her for coffee.

I said, "Yea, for sure, just give me an hour to get up and get ready."

I met her at a *Second Cup* on Lakeshore near my place. She was a mess. The guy she had been seeing, borrowed her car and never came back, the cops were after her for unpaid parking tickets this guy was accumulating on her license plate, and the car dealership was after her to continue making the payments on a car she no longer had possession of. She was so hurt and humiliated.

All I could do was let her cry on my shoulder. I didn't have any experience dealing with a situation like this. Then my mom called me and she was upset, she asked if I could come home and go for a walk with her. What is going on, I thought. I'm sitting here with Betsy crying, and my mother the toughest woman I know, who never leans on me decides for the first time in her life to ask me to be at her side. I said I'd be home shortly that I couldn't just get up and leave Betsy like that. I didn't think it could be anything serious that my mom was going through. I dropped Betsy off about an hour later after she calmed down, by the time I got home my mom was in bed. I felt bad. The next day she said don't worry about it, that was it.

It was the beginning of a new baseball season; I'd just arrived at work. My hair was in its natural curly state, I was in a hurry after going to the gym so I just threw some clips in it, and off to work I went. I was brunette naturally but at the time, my hair was full of blonde highlights. On this day, my big frizzy natural curls worked in my favor, they caught the eye of the hottie that was dining in our establishment.

I was guzzling water by the bar to rehydrate, and talking to the girls at work. Suddenly, I looked up and saw the hottie walking through the restaurant toward the back exit that leads to the elevators to the stadium. He was not Canadian. No way. I'd never seen a guy from here that looked like that. He had on dark jeans, a red t-shirt, a red headband, and perfect white sneakers, not a mark on them. Everything matched. I was looking at him; my eyes were following him out the door. He was looking back but no one was making a move.

Just as he was about to exit Christine, shouted, "He wants your number."

He stopped dead in his tracks and walked over to me.

"Hey, your coworker said you wanted to meet me. What's your name?" he said with a heavy southern accent.

"I'm Lily. Where are you from?" I asked.

"Texas. Houston Texas," he replied.

Of course, you are, I thought, everything from Texas is bigger. His fingers and hands were huge, thick, and long. He told me his name was Mark Bishop, and that he was the starting pitcher for the Houston Astros baseball team.

"Oh sorry. That's embarrassing. I guess I should've known that."

He didn't seem to care, we chatted for a minute then he quickly took down my telephone number and made his way down to the field.

After work at around midnight when I went to my locker to get my stuff and head home, I checked my phone and found a bunch of missed phone calls. Mark had called me at least six times after the game up until midnight. Just as I was about to curse at my bad luck from missing his calls because I'd left my cell phone in my locker, it rang.

"Lily, where have you been? Listen, I have to meet some of my teammates at a club for about an hour, can I call you after," asked Mark.

"Sure," I replied.

After turned into two thirty in the morning. When he asked me to come over I didn't think, I just went because it had been over two years since I'd had any type of human contact with a man outside of work.

When we talked, he didn't want to go into his past. We kissed passionately that's all. He wasn't pressuring me to go any further, which I respected him for. He was a good kisser. We eventually fell asleep, well actually he fell asleep on top of me, all six feet two of him. At 220 lbs. of solid muscle, he was heavy. I couldn't move, breath, or fall asleep. Except my extremities, of course they were numbing from my circulation being cut off.

When he woke up in the morning, I saw his perfect naked body walk from the bed to the bathroom. Wow, he had the most perfect ass I have ever seen. He came back to bed, and started to make a move to fool around. What can I say, I did need a first base coach in life, I gave in. He was sexy and turned me on. He didn't seem like a perverted pig, I felt safe. Again, I hoped for the best, that it wouldn't be just about sex. It wasn't for me. I would've been happy just leaving it at cuddling for the night. Is it so much to ask of me, that I find someone I mean something to? When I was lying in bed alone for those last two years, I didn't feel like I mattered to this world. At least for those brief moments when I'm in someone's arms I feel like my existence matters to someone. That need just never went away it consumed me.

Mark walked me outside, gave me a big hug, I melted into him. His skin felt like buttery silk. I got into my car and drove myself home.

The next morning, I awoke to my cell phone ringing. It was Mark.

"Lily. I can't stop thinking about you. Come meet me in Texas," said Mark.

"What, when?" I asked.

"As soon as possible, I made you a reservation for a flight under your name at the airport. Will you come?" he asked.

"Yes, I'll be there," I said.

"Great. I can't wait to see you. I got to go. Bye," said Mark.

The first thing I did was call into work and use one of my sick days. I made up an excuse that I had a family emergency. There was no way I was going to pass up this opportunity. If there was even a remote chance of finding true love with Mark I had to go there to find out. I knew if I didn't I would have regretted it for the rest of my life.

There I was on a plane heading to Texas drinking a diet Coke and reading the latest fashion magazine. Wishing I hadn't decided to drown my sorrows by stuffing my face with that big piece of cheesecake last night. I didn't have many outfits to choose from. I grabbed a pair of jeans, a hoody and threw them in my suitcase with all my toiletries. If there's one thing I knew about the States, it was that they had a lot more choices in clothing. I was hoping I'd get a chance to shop and find something new to wear when I got there. I have never been to Houston before and wondered what it might be like. For some reason, I pictured tall, strong masculine, herding cattlemen, with big cowboy hats, and old-fashioned southern manners.

The flight attendant suddenly interrupted my daydreaming by forcefully shaking my shoulder.

"Hey. Are you listening to me? You should be in the proper crash-landing position," she said.

"Sorry. Run that by me again," I said.

"Didn't you hear the captain? One of the flaps isn't working. Now prepare yourself, I need you to sit in the crash-landing position," she demanded, walking away very upset.

Instinctively I looked out my window and low and

behold, I just happened to be on the exact side by the wing where I could see the flap wasn't moving. I quickly slid the window cover down and looked straight ahead in absolute fear. The dinging sound from the seatbelt sign flashed in front of my eyes. Are you fucking kidding me? I had a family that loved me and I was on a plane going to see a man I barely knew who I probably shouldn't be going to see. When was I going to smarten up? Doing things out of loneliness was only getting me into trouble. Now my plane might crash and burst into flames. If I died right there and then I would have been devastated because I never found true love. Some people believe if you die and have unfinished business you end up coming back and living the exact same life over again, until you figure out what you were supposed to learn the first time around. I sure as hell didn't want to die and go through another life of being single for a fucking decade. What was I not getting, what do I need to learn to fix this? I just spent two years alone, what is it, I stopped sleeping with men, nothing changed, give me a helping hand with this incessant life of solitude would you God? I am always left with no friends and no love interest, and at the same time, you send me signs that I'm not supposed to fill that void in life with these hot men that come along once in a blue moon. Why is this happening to me?

After I heard the flight attendant explain that without the flaps to slow us down we could run out of runway, which could cause the plane to hit rough ground and the gas tanks could rupture. Thus, causing the plane to burst into flames, I flipped the blind up looked out the window and saw at least a dozen fire trucks with their flashing lights lined up and down the run way waiting for us. That's when I knew it was time to smarten up. The first thing I did was strap my purse around my neck. This eighty-year-old lady sitting beside me turned her head stared right at me opened her big mouth revealing what few little yellow teeth she had left, and yelled.

"We were just told no personal belongings allowed if we have to do an emergency evacuation."

"Listen lady, don't mess with me right now. I'm having a midlife crisis. If I make it out of this alive I want my makeup with me. So, shut up and mind your own business," I said.

I wasn't normally that mean but honestly this was a very stressful situation. I slid the window cover back down and went into full crash-landing position. A voice over the P.A. came on loud and clear.

"This is the captain speaking. We are now making

our descent. Please keep your seatbelts securely fastened and remain in the position the flight attendants instructed you on."

    They say life flashes before your eyes during a near death experience but not for me, not this time anyway. I felt numb. The sound of the wheels squealing didn't even faze me because I couldn't feel a thing. I looked over at the other passengers to see their reactions. I saw a couple holding each other's hand kissing each other as if it was their last embrace. An executive praying aloud promising he'd be a better person if he lived to see another day. A young boy was bent over crying. It seemed everyone else felt some sort of emotion except me. Was I going into shock? When the screeching sound of the airplane touching the runway traveled its way into my ears, my nerves came back to me and I began shaking all over. I lifted the blind, looked out my window and saw smoke coming from the tires as the plane jumped a beat trying to make a successful complete stop. When I started to hear people screaming that's when I couldn't take it anymore shutting my eyes and waiting for fate to do the rest. When the noise stopped, I opened my eyes and saw people clapping their hands. By some miracle, we made it. When you've survived something like that, it makes you realize that life is short, it could end at any moment. I'd rather be known for being a good person than someone rude. The first thing I did was apologize to the old woman for yelling at her; there was no excuse for that.

After collecting my bags, I still felt emotionally distraught. Directly in front of me was a small airport bar. I needed a drink to calm my nerves. The female bartender, wearing horn-rimmed eyeglasses greeted me with a thin smile, not the comfort or warm southern hospitality I was hoping for at that moment, I guess I was going to have to rely on the alcohol for that.

"What can I get you?" she asked.

My eyes darted straight toward the first bottle I saw.

"Whiskey, a shot of whiskey, straight up," I said.

The bartender gave me a judgmental look as if to say whiskey was a man's drink. I didn't care I needed something strong to help calm my nerves, I wanted to feel normal when I saw Mark. "You look nervous," said the bartender. I swallowed down the whiskey and gave her a twenty-dollar bill. "Keep the change," I said. The drink only cost five bucks but I was in a generous mood. "Thanks ma'am." said the bartender. And don't call me ma'am, I'm not an old lady, I thought but didn't say, I realized it was just a southern expression. I kept my mouth shut, which most people should do, and just kept on walking.

As I wandered outside with my luggage in hand I noticed a man in a black suit, was holding up a sign with my name on it. "That's me, I'm Lily Monroe," I said. "Do you have any identification?" asked the chauffeur. As soon as I showed the man my passport, he took my bags, and we drove off in a black limo. Looking out the car window, I saw a completely different Texas than I imagined on the airplane. Yes, there were a few people wearing cowboy hats but for the most part everyone looked the same as they did back home. What drew me in were the tall skyscrapers that went on as far as the eye could see, obviously connected to the major oil tycoons in the area. There were huge mansions; the homes looked like old estate houses not anything like the houses we build in Ontario. They had thick tall pillars outlining the huge doors that were the front entrance to the home. I had no idea where I was going or what the agenda was. I was going with the flow just trying to enjoy my comfortable limousine ride.

The vehicle stopped out front of the baseball stadium. "I should have guessed," I said aloud. "Mister Bishop told me to give you this," said the chauffeur. He handed me a sealed white envelope. I eagerly tore open the envelope to discover a baseball ticket and a letter.

Dear Lily,

Sorry I couldn't meet you at the airport today. We had a game tonight, as you know I can't call in sick like you can. It doesn't quite work that way in my profession. I promise to make it up to you after the game. We'll have an amazing night out; I'll show you how we do it up Texas style. I hope you enjoy the game. I've arranged for you to order any food or drinks on me, just show your ticket and everything will be taken care of. Please leave your bags with the driver. He will drop it off at my condo.

Thinking of you,
Mark

I was on cloud nine. Life could not get any better than this. Nothing could wipe the smile off my face. I got out of the car and made my way inside the stadium. The usher personally escorted me to my seat that was directly behind home plate. So far, Mark was making a stellar impression on me; he sure knew how to treat a lady. I know it was a mistake having sex with him right away; thank God, he was giving us a chance to get to know each other.

My heart was beating faster than I've ever felt before. I kept looking at the letter reminding myself just how lucky I was.

I was so happy I'd made it there for the beginning of the game, I was there to see Mark approach the pitcher's mound, and throw his first pitch for the night. Right before he threw it he looked directly at me and winked. Mark was a true romantic; the seat I was sitting in had a direct view of him. Throughout the game, I kept seeing him glance in my direction. The attraction we had for each other was so intense you could have cut the air between us with a knife. He had a great game that night, almost every time a batter came up to the plate, he would strike them out. I liked to think my presence gave him that extra boost of confidence. I had a light snack in case he'd made dinner plans, the players always eat after a game. I had salad with grilled chicken, and some mineral water. I certainly didn't need alcohol I was drunk on love.

The Astros kicked ass that night and beat Kansas City Royals eight to five. It came down to the final inning where Mark threw a curve ball while the bases were loaded and struck the Royals hitter out. It felt great to watch him win a game like that.

Afterwards, Mark and I grabbed a cab to a

destination unknown, unknown to me of course. The whole city was new to me. I plunked myself down on his lap wrapping my arms around him and gave him a kiss.

"I'm here yay! Great game," I said trying to break the ice.

"It was nothing. I'm just glad you came Lily," said Mark.

"Me too," I said.

We both gazed into each other's eyes and within seconds, we were making out. Then I felt his leg rub up against mine, even with a driver in the front seat we still couldn't keep our hands off each other. It took everything in me not to rip his clothes off in the cab. When the cab stopped, I could see that we were outside a bar that looked a little rustic. It wasn't the upscale restaurant I'd anticipated, but I had faith in his choices. Mark grabbed me in close, it was an intense hug, we continued kissing. I wanted him so bad, I could feel his erection pressing up against my thigh through his jeans. It felt great knowing he wanted me as much as I wanted him. After twenty minutes of making out we decided to break our embrace and go inside the bar for a drink. The exterior of the building had a glowing yellow marquee sign that read *drinks in here, with an arrow pointing at the entrance*. The pale-yellow light coming through the glass windows made me wonder as to what lay waiting for us inside. The first thing I noticed was the beautiful mirror above the bar, framed in solid bronze. The next thing my eyes were drawn to were the gorgeous chocolate brown leather bar stools that looked like they were made from an old saddle. I loved the look of the hardwood floors; next to the brick walls, it gave it a rustic industrial look. I noticed instantly that there were very few women inside. I guess the south is still segregated, and discriminating. This looked like a man's hang out. Everyone seemed to be staring at us; it made me a little uneasy. I pulled myself closer to Mark and held onto his arm. We took a seat at the bar.

Of course, being that it was Texas there was your typical steer head hanging by the bar, and a Texas state flag hung over a huge pool table in the far corner. Looking around the bar it seemed there were twenty or so patrons that came from the rough neck of the woods.

"Are you sure you got the right place?" I said in a hushed tone.

"Trust me. You're going to love this place. Lily, the food is amazing, the music is great, and I wanted to introduce you to a good friend of mine," said Mark.

"My man, how's it hanging?" said the bartender.

They fist bumped before Mark spoke, "Lily, this smiling fool is Jack."

"Pleasure to meet you."

Jack had a constant grin on his face from ear to ear with a fair Irish complexion, and devilish blue piercing eyes.

"Judging by your accent you ain't from around these parts are y'all?"

"No, JD. She's from Toronto, Canada. Lily works at a restaurant inside the SkyDome, where we play ball. That's how we met," said Mark.

"Right on. Right on. So, what can I get for you two love birds," asked Jack.

"I'll have a Bud. Lily order whatever you want," said Mark.

"Okay. I'll have a Grey Goose and diet Coke," I replied.

Mark and Jack looked at each other and smiled.

"What's wrong?" I asked.

"I don't get asked for that too often in these parts. They serve plenty of that downtown where the other ball players hang out, ain't that the truth Bishop," said Jack.

"You know it JD," said Mark.

"Wait a minute. If your name is Jack, then why

does he call you JD?"

"Ever since I've met him he always liked his Jack Daniels. Hell, he probably drank the stuff right out of his baby bottle. All the regulars here know he is a JD man there's been plenty nights he sat down and shared a few drinks with his customers. So, the name JD stuck," said Mark.

JD snapped his fingers.

"I got it! Lily have you ever tried a Sazerac?" asked JD.

"What's a Sazerac?" I replied.

"Watch the master and you shall see," said JD.

The first thing he grabbed were two rock glass, one at room temperature and one thoroughly chilled. JD produced a single sugar cube, which he carefully dropped into the room temperature glass along with a few drops of water and muddled the sugar into a fine pulp. Next came a handful of tiny ice cubes that went inside the glass. Rye whiskey and Peychaud's bitters were then poured into the glass and stirred slowly with a metal spoon. JD rolled a few drops of Absinthe around the chilled glass until the inside was thoroughly coated, pouring off the excess. He then took a strainer and strained the room temperature glass into the chilled glass and garnished it with a lemon twist. The vibrant red color from the drink reminded me of cherry brandy or sweet vermouth, the smell had a strong medicine quality. JD took out a bottle of Jack Daniel's and poured himself a glass and grabbed Mark's bottle of beer.

"This Lily is the holiest of southern cocktails, the Sazerac. Legend has it the cocktail originated in New Orleans but everyone knows Texans make em' best," said JD.

Mark raised his beer into the air.

"To your first night in Texas and to the most beautiful girl I've ever seen," said Mark.

We clanked glasses in a celebratory salute as if I was one of the boys. I was having the time of my life. It felt great to be a part of someone's life.

The Sazerac tasted sweet, spicy and herbal. Almost like a smoky rye. I choked it down fast due to how strong it was. The drink was not for wimps like me that like a lot of mix with their alcohol.

"Whew, that shit'll grow hair on your chest," I said after I took my first sip. Everyone laughed.

"I guess that means she likes it," laughed JD.

"A toast to my new drinking partner Lily from Canada," we all laughed and cheered.

I chugged the rest of mine, to end my pain quickly.

"He's crazy isn't he," I said to Mark.

"Yep, the craziest, that's why we love him. JD's one of my oldest, closest friends. I come here after most of our home games because it's the one place where most people don't recognize me, or care who I am," said Mark.

"Let's go sit at a more private table," said Mark

"Lead the way," I replied. We got up from our bar stools and walked over to the jukebox. Mark smiled at me as I flipped through the musical choices.

"Find anything good?" he asked.

"You pick," I said.

Mark picked a hip-hop remix of the Bee Gees classic, *Stayin Alive* by N-Trance. As soon as the track hit the speakers, the room became electric with everyone jumping on the dance floor. Mark started to strut his stuff pulling off some John Travolta disco moves, and then twirled me around in circles. He was so into it, which cracked me up, I couldn't believe how much fun I was having, it felt like I was living a dream.

We started grinding on the dance floor, which led to us being the only couple on the dance floor making out. Suddenly, our kiss got interrupted when he got a tap on the shoulder from a group of young guys dressed in Kansas City Royals Jerseys.

"Hey. Are you Mark Bishop the pitcher for the Astros?"

"Yeah. That's me. Look I'm kind of busy with my girl now so if you don't mind giving us a little space I'd appreciate it. "

"Yo man. Tonight's game was not cool. I had three hundred bucks riding on that game," said one of the Jersey boys.

"I'm sorry to hear that. What can I tell you, maybe you should stick to just watching the game next time instead," said Mark.

"You think this is funny," said another Jersey boy.

"Now listen here," said Mark.

"No, you listen. Maybe next game you won't play at all," said a Jersey boy.

"That's not going to happen," said Mark. Just then one of the boys pulled out a switchblade. A group of patrons walked up toward us.

"Don't worry, Bishop. We got your back," said one of the regulars.

"Wanna bet," said Jersey boy #1 as he punched Mark hard in the mouth making his lower lip bleed. That's when a full out bar fight ensued. Fists were flying everywhere. JD immediately pulled down a gate covering his bottles on a shelf and locked it up. For some reason, I had a feeling this wasn't the first bar fight that happened here. Mark knew he had to get out, his career depended on it. Fighting with these punks, could easily cost him a season ending injury or worse a suspension from the league. I stood far away in the corner of the room trying not to get involved. Until I saw two Kansas boys rushing Mark from behind, he was defenseless.

I grabbed a beer bottle and smashed it over one of the Kansas boy's heads, then yelled, "Mark look out." The rest of the customers ganged up on the two Kansas boys, which gave Mark and I just enough time to get the hell out of there before the cops showed up. Just as we were leaving, Mark took out his wallet and threw JD five hundred dollars.

"I'm really sorry about this JD," said Mark.

"Hey, I'm the one who should be sorry; I gotta be more careful who I let in here. Can't afford to lose my favorite customer. At least no alcohol got busted," JD said laughing trying to make light of the situation. You could tell he was pissed.

"Now get out of here before the cops come, and trust me this won't happen again. I'm going to tighten up on security," said JD, still smiling.

*** ***

Thirty minutes later, we were back at Mark's condo. Thank God, he made it out without a scratch on him, aside from his cut lip, but that's nothing compared to losing his pitching arm for a season. I leaned over and gave him a gentle kiss to ease his nerves. He'd fought hard to be in the big leagues; he has been plagued with numerous injuries in all his past seasons, plus he'd been sent down to the minors. He was finally having a career-changing season; he certainly didn't need anyone to mess that up. I could tell it was weighing heavy on his mind.

He kissed me on the forehead and said, "I'm sorry babe. Maybe we should just call it a night."

Then he grabbed me picked me up and carried me into the bedroom. We made love; it seemed more meaningful than the first time we were together. He held me so close the entire night after we finished, that's how we slept for the rest of the night, in a tight embrace. I couldn't help but feel bad for him.

"It's not fair that you're a target for people that could care less if they ruin your life," I whispered in his ear.

"I'm just glad you were here," said Mark.

He pulled me in closer put his hands on my face and planted an everlasting kiss that swallowed me whole.

Yes, there is a difference between having sex and making love, much like the difference between a job and a career. A job is just a job; a career is doing something you love.

Chapter Seventeen
The Morning After

I awoke to the sound of clinking glassware. Mark was already dressed in a gray t-shirt and dark boot-cut jeans. A TV tray rested beside my bed with a plate of pancakes, whipped butter, hash browns, scrambled eggs, bacon, Texas toast, a cup of coffee and a glass of freshly squeezed orange juice.

"Breakfast is served," said Mark.

"You made all this for me?" I asked.

"Well, who else would it be for? You know me I sure like to eat, and whenever I do something I do it right," said Mark.

"This is so sweet, oh my God, thank you so much,

there definitely is enough here for both of us, I can't believe you made all my favorites. How did you know?"

"As soon as we're done eating, we gotta hit the road," said Mark. "Why, what's going on, where are we going?" I asked.

"You ever been horseback riding?" asked Mark. I nodded yes.

"Well I hope you liked it, because that's where we're headed."

I put my arms around his neck and pulled him back into bed. We kissed, made love. The breakfast ended up on the floor. When we finished, we were soaked with sweat, we jumped in the shower together, got ready, stopped for coffee on the way, took it to go with a multigrain bagel, and off we went. He said since my flight leaves at nine tonight he wanted to have as much fun as possible. I was so glad they didn't have a game that night. I sat back and just enjoyed the ride.

✱✱✱ ✱✱✱

What Mark failed to tell me was our horseback-riding trail was a four-hour drive from Houston in a city called Southlake Texas. Even though there were a few trails to choose from that were much closer Mark chose Southlake since it was the cream of the crop in all of Texas.

Our guide, Austin, a thin sixty-year-old man sporting a white straw cowboy hat, red plaid shirt and dirt-encrusted blue jeans greeted us with a smile. There was a faint smell of manure in the air, mixed with straw. Our guide looked like he'd spent most of his life enjoying the great outdoors. He had that sun-aged leather looking skin, accompanied with the deep lines of someone who'd enjoyed his life, there was a Clint Eastwood star quality to him. Austin showed us to our horses. Mark's was a gray-colored horse appropriately named Dusty while mine was a beautiful white horse called Pegasus. Its hair was blond and she moved so gracefully I was in awe. That soon wore off once I tried getting on the horse; the saddle hadn't been fastened properly so I fell back and landed on my butt. There was sand, and dirt all over me.

"Is this your first time getting on a horse?" asked Austin.

"No, but it's been a long time," I said, blushing.

Mark was looking down at me from his horse and laughing.

"Don't you worry Lily, he'll fasten that saddle on tight and you'll be just fine," said Mark.

Austin got off his horse, fixed the saddle, then instructed me on how to properly mount a horse. I followed his instructions and managed to climb up onto Pegasus just fine. Unfortunately, before I had my left foot properly secured Pegasus took off into a gallop, I was sliding all over the place, and hanging on for dear life. Pegasus raced toward the fence outside the stables and jumped right over it. Just then I heard another set of hooves coming toward me. It was Mark and his horse galloping up behind us to rescue me. I could feel my fingers starting to get numb from hanging onto the reins so tight, because my body had shifted so far left I was dangling from her side. That's when Mark and his horse caught up with Pegasus side by side.

"Lily, grab my hand," yelled Mark.

As I reached out to grab his arm my body plunged toward the ground. All I could see were the horse's feet that just barely missed my head.

"Lily, I'm going to pull you up on the count of three. One, two, three," said Mark.

He forcefully grabbed my body as I pulled my right foot from the saddle. He lifted me up in the air with all his strength and placed me on the back of his horse, while

Austin charged forward to stop Pegasus.

"You saved my life," I said.

Mark was my knight in shining armor that day.

"Anything for a special lady like you," replied Mark as he leaned in for a gentle kiss.

My pounding heart was immediately calmed, and filled with a warm feeling inside. I knew I was falling in love with him. Nothing was said, but I think deep down we both knew there was something magical between us.

After my nerves subsided, Mark convinced me to get back up on Pegasus and give her a second chance. I'm glad he did, because the trail ride was incredible. Austin led us through some marshland that ended at a beautiful lake. The gray overcast sky brought out the natural colors of the intense pine green from the bushes, and the cream-colored sand, against the azure blue coming off the lake made this whole view breathtaking. Our guide Austin suggested our horses take a rest in the lake to cool off from the hot sun and politely wandered down the beach to give us some private time.

"Thank you for bringing me here, I really needed this in my life," I said.

"What do you mean?" asked Mark.

"Every woman needs romance and adventure in her

life. Otherwise, we start to question why we're here. Is that too deep? I know I'm too deep sometimes, and most people aren't into that."

"I just think that one of the problems with most relationships is that they forget to do fun things together, like going horseback riding, bowling, dancing, you know things that make you reconnect with the person you are with, on a romantic level. Maybe some marriages could be saved if they made time to go on interesting dates instead of falling into a routine of work, cooking, cleaning, kids, rest, and repeat. I'm talking too much aren't I," I said.

"Not at all, I try to enjoy the moment, and not worry what the future holds, that's my philosophy. I just go with the flow and see where it takes me," said Mark.

I slowly turned my head away from Mark shedding a tear. "What's wrong? Was it something I said?" asked Mark.

"No, no, no. In fact, you're saying all the right things, it's just all my life I've dated liars, cheaters and thieves, you name it I've dated it. You have old-fashioned manners, and know how to treat a woman, and I've been hoping to find that my whole life," I said.

"Lily I'm not going to lie, these last two days have been great, I've had a lot of fun with you, but I'm on the road a lot," said Mark.

The words I didn't want to hear, that dreaded speech. I pretended it was cool, I knew the drill.

"I know, I know. I won't be able to see you again for a while. I'm embarrassed. I'm usually a lot cooler at hiding my true feelings," I said.

"I'll be back in Toronto soon I'll see you the next time we're in town," said Mark.

"That would be nice," I said.

Mark gave me a nice long kiss. The setting was the epitome of romance it made me wish this day would never end, but as the golden sun began to set, casting an orange tinge along the skyline I knew it was time to go.

After our deep long kiss, Mark looked me in the eye like I was the love of his life, then quickly realized after glancing at his watch that my flight was leaving in a few short hours. We thanked Austin for his hospitality and Mark drove me straight to the airport. As my plane took off I decided that he was hiding his true feelings, and how much he did care about me, and let my mind wonder creating a beautiful picture of our bright future together. I realized I hadn't bought one single souvenir. Instead, I gained memories that would last a lifetime; and that was something money could never buy.

Chapter Eighteen
It Takes Two to Tango

When I arrived home from my weekend trip, my life was turned upside down. Still floating on cloud nine from the amazing time I had in Houston with Mark, I was soon brought back to reality the minute I walked through the door at work. Meet Owen Baker, a five foot eight bully, with a big bowling ball, beer belly. He looked like he might be due any day. He'd been working at J10 for over fifteen years now, upon my return I was delivered the horrible news he'd been promoted to a managerial position, assistant GM to be exact. He had more cockiness than brains, a reputation of having a very bad temper, and a nasty habit of targeting the new girl in hopes of fulfilling his perverted sexual needs. What made him even more of a creep was that he was married, had a brand-new baby girl, and in his mid-forties was still *trying to* chase every piece of ass he could get his hands on. Owen thought he was hot shit, I have no idea why, he was not. When I first started at J10, Owen tried to put the moves on me, I quickly shot him down, and he'd been bitter ever since. Not only was I not vaguely interested in him but when my coworkers informed me that he was a newlywed, I was disgusted. I felt sorry for his wife and child. I made sure I kept any dialog with him, strictly about business and only spoke to him when necessary. Now that Owen had become my manager, I would be forced to speak to him more often. This did not help my work environment at all. I was already dealing with most of my coworkers being jealous of me, due to guys regularly leaving me huge tips. It wasn't me who bragged about it either. I was smart enough to keep my mouth shut, I didn't need to contribute to any animosity toward me. But they would sneak behind my back and find out how much I made by checking my sales report at the end of every night. The guys I worked with were acting up just as much as the girls. Everyone seemed aggravated ever since I started hanging out with professional ball players. By this time I knew a few famous ones and they were coming in and asking for me when I wasn't there or requesting my section when I was. There was nothing I could do to stop people from finding out I knew these guys. Apparently, this was driving everyone mad. In the meantime, I was concerned about Mark, my loyalty was to him and all this other attention didn't mean a thing to me. It didn't matter to me that he was living in the States, when it came to the possibility of true love I would never let distance stand in my way. I went from being the favorite which came with several perks like making my own schedule, picking my days off, paid trips at the end of every season to other J10's across the border in New York which included dinner, and spending money while we were there. To being on the new general manager's hit list, and Owen was more than happy to join him. Owen was out to get me, he whispered in my ear that he would be doing my schedule from now on, I would no longer be able to choose my shifts or have the days off I wanted because he'd been with the company for over fifteen years and he didn't have that privilege, so why should I? I'm sure it had nothing to do with the fact that I had refused to sleep with him numerous times. Everyone decided I thought I was too good for them because they weren't famous. It was ridiculous; I wasn't interested in the fame. I was interested in the guys I met that were fun, smart, fit, and attractive.

They had a positive energy that would draw anyone in, it was that simple. However, I could defend my integrity until I'm blue in the face, in the end people will decide their own truths. I found out years later that some of my coworkers started talking shit about me to management. They said I was speaking badly about them behind their back. Of course, everyone believed whatever they heard and never thought for a minute that these people were full of shit. Not one single person bothered to ask me if I was talking about them. I had no idea what was going on at the time, I could just feel the tension at work, and when the managers started picking on me I had no idea why. As far as I knew I was being picked on for no legitimate reason. It was like high school all over again, gossip central. We live in a day and age where bullying continues well after high school. Yet, they still don't teach you in school how to stop it. That's why there's all this outrage about '13 Reasons Why'. People are killing themselves over bullying and no one's doing a damn thing to put an end to it. I couldn't believe that it still existed in adult life. I wasn't interested in brown nosing or a popularity contest, I just wanted to do my job, be left the fuck alone, pay my bills and go on auditions in hope of getting closer to my dreams of becoming a successful actress.

When pretty much everyone is out to get you it's difficult to hide the affect it has on you. I had to keep a facade up that everything was fine. I pretended that nothing they were doing was getting to me, but deep down I was upset that this is where I was in life. I was bad mouthed, hit, tripped, given wrong food orders, my food and drink orders would go missing and not get made, then I'd have to argue with the kitchen and the bar to get them, then my customers would be pissed off because it took me so long to bring their order to the table. I was being sexually harassed by my manager, I was a total mess. Every day when I walked into work I felt sick to my stomach. I was a nervous wreck, but I had bills to pay I couldn't just up and quit my job, that's not who I am, that wouldn't be responsible or fair. At night, I would lie in bed praying to God for help. One night a story I'd been told about someone filing a law suit called constructive dismissal came back to me. This person said that they were harassed to the point they had to quit their job, and when they took their boss to court, they won. I started taking notes of everything that was said and done to me. I wrote down dates and times. When the baseball season ended, I quit, took my ten pages of notes and found myself a lawyer. I figured God made me remember that story for a reason. It was the right thing to do, defend myself, and take these fuckers to court for harassment.

    I arrived at the courtroom in a black suit with a large folder in my hand. I wanted to make sure I looked conservative, and professional. For the judge to take me seriously. I may not agree with the fact that we live in a society that judge's people based on their appearance but the reality is we do, and I was willing to play the part. When Owen walked in my stomach turned into knots. I was nervous as hell on the inside but there was no way I was going to show anything but a pillar of strength on the outside. Just the thought of facing Owen knowing how bad his temper is and now that his job was being jeopardized, he'd be even more angry, scared the hell out of me, my heart was racing. I had seen him lose his temper it was not a pleasant sight; he had brought several girls to tears. I would not be one of them. I made sure I appeared calm, and in control. He couldn't even look me in the eye. I walked up and sat next to my lawyer. I had my detailed notes, a signed affidavit from one of my coworkers who had experienced the same harassment, I had my shit together and I knew I was doing the right thing. No one should have to work under someone like that. The judge entered the room and sat down with such detachment I wondered if he was on their side already. Looking over the documents in front of him the judge put on his reading glasses and the proceedings began.

"The case between Lily Monroe and J10. Lily Monroe, please take the stand," said the judge.

"Thank you, your honor," I replied.

"Miss Monroe please kindly state your case?"

In some ways, I was glad Owen was in the room; his presence was all the inspiration I needed to ensure everyone knew the truth about how horrible it was to work with him. I finally had the chance to expose him for the abusive person that he was.

"Let me state the facts. What I am about to tell the courts is normally considered as hearsay but because I have signed witness statements you will find this to not be the case. For the last few weeks ever since Owen Baker has become general manager I have been mistreated at work and harassed. I have been badmouthed, tripped, hit, injured, given wrong food orders resulting in angry customers and lack of customer service but worst of all, was the sexual harassment from Owen himself. I would like to state to the courts that Owen is a married man," I said.

"Is this true?" asked the judge.

"Yes, that's correct."

"Please proceed," said the judge.

"Thank you. If you would please refer to the signed affidavit," I said being cut off by the judge.

"Look, I'm going to get straight to the point. I have reviewed all the documents Miss Monroe has submitted as well as Mr. Bakers. I find Monroe's statements to be true. Just to be sure, I would like to call Christine Miller to the stand. You may step down Miss Monroe."

I walked over to my side of the table and gave a slight smile to Owen. Christine was my ace in the hole. She was the only friend I had at J10. Judging by Owens pale face, and blank expression, he must have been quite surprised that I had a witness. Even though Christine was afraid of losing her job she still promised to stand up for me in court, her presence there was a way of standing up for all the girls working at J10 and a big screw you to Owen.

"Miss Miller, would you please tell the courts what you have witnessed in regards to Miss Monroe?" asked the judge.

"Sure thing, several times I've seen Owen hitting on Lily. He tries to rub up against her, he's grabbed her ass. I saw him walk behind her and trip her; she fell to the ground and twisted her wrist. She had to be off work for at least ten days after that. He makes disgusting sexual comments to her. She tried to get help from head office and made an anonymous call, then things got even worse. He cut her shifts back, gave her the worst sections, he has cost her lots of money over that last year. Let's see, oh yes, the most recent thing he's done is refusing to give her the days off she needed to spend time with her parents, something that he knew was very important to her. She had those days off for years, and it hadn't caused any problem in the running of the restaurant prior to him doing the schedule. He actually admitted he was trying to make her life a living hell," said Christine.

"Thank you, Miss Miller," said the judge.

"That's not all," said Christine.

"Oh? Please proceed."

"Ever since I started working at J10, I have witnessed him hitting on several of my female coworkers, asking them out for drinks, and when they don't respond he finds stupid reasons to reprimand them at work, and then screams at the top of his lungs at them in front of everyone. It is terrifying. He came right out and said, I've been trying to fuck you for five years now, to Lily. Considering this man is married it makes me sick to my stomach the way he conducts himself," said Christine. "Thank you, Miss Miller that will be all," replied the judge.

"Mister Baker, do you have anything to say?" said the judge.

"Yes. I may have flirted with a few of my colleagues but I have in no way shape or form did what the two of them are accusing me of." said Owen.

"Mister Baker, do you have any evidence, or character witnesses to back up your defense?" asked the judge.

"No, I don't," replied Owen.

"Since you have no witnesses or any burden of proof to validate your innocence it is under my discretion to decide who in this court is telling the truth. I believe Miss Monroe to be the one in the right and you Mr. Baker to be guilty of her accusations. Before I pass judgment, I would like to pass on a word of advice. I have been married to my wife for over fifteen years. At no time, have I ever jeopardized that relationship by harassing women I work with. The fact that you Mister Baker seem to have no conscience for what is right or wrong troubles me not only for yourself but for your wife. At the end of the day, we must live with the consequences from our actions. My advice for you Mister Baker is to get some counseling for your temper, and your marriage," said the judge.

Now as much as I'd like to tell you what happened

next, the only thing I can say is that I won my case. I had to sign an official document swearing to never publicly disclose the details of my settlement. I can also tell you that both Christine and I went out to celebrate. I honestly felt as one chapter in my life was ending, another one had just begun with Mark. Unfortunately, that wasn't the case. Yes, they had to give me my job back. At this point you're probably wondering why I would want to go back, and the answer is simple really, my illness made it difficult for me to make a living elsewhere due to my physical limitations. I couldn't carry heavy trays, I couldn't climb staircases, long shifts were difficult, mornings and forty-hour work weeks were impossible. I had to make the most money I could in the least amount of time, and that combined with all my other restrictions made it hard to work just anywhere. Owen did stop sexually harassing me at work but the mind games, and gossip between the staff continued. Hardly anyone would talk to me in fear I might take him or her to court. So much for sticking up for yourself it didn't solve my problems at all. I am still proud of myself for going through with the court case, it just doesn't make sense that defending myself caused more harm than good.

For the next couple of months, I tried to ignore what was going on at work until one day I felt a sharp pain in my stomach. At first, I thought it was stress related but when I got home I did some calculations, and realized the possibility that it was something else. I bought a pregnancy test. My suspicions were confirmed. Looking back now I can't believe I didn't take that magic pill so many women use. I was having such a great time with Mark I had forgotten how risky we were when we slept together. Coming home to a shit storm at work didn't help matters and before I knew it, I had this dilemma upon me. There was no doubt in my mind whose baby this was. He was the only man I'd been with, in two years. The million-dollar question was how would Mark feel? I didn't want to lose what we had over a baby. What if Mark wanted it? So many questions raced through my mind. After a horrible night's sleep and thinking about it nonstop day and night, I finally got the nerve to tell him.

"Lily. How's it going?" said Mark.

"I'm pregnant," I just blurted it out, I'm not sure why.

"What did you say?" he asked.

I repeated myself with very little enthusiasm. There was a moment of silence on the other end of the line.

"Why do you sound so upset? Why would that be bad news, I love kids," said Mark.

I was shocked, excuse me, come again. Isn't this when you say I knew it; I knew you were a gold digger?

"What's the plan, what are we going to do," asked Mark.

"I don't really want this baby. I never really wanted children," all I heard was silence, then he slammed the phone against the wall.

I stood there motionless listening to dial tone on my phone as the line went dead. I couldn't believe what just happened, I felt horrible.

When the pre-recorded message came on, "Please hang up and try your call again, please hang up, this is a recording," I picked up the receiver and hung up the phone.

There was no way I could go into work the next day, I had to deal with this right away so I took the day off from work, setup an appointment with the clinic and sat in bed crying myself to sleep.

Chapter Nineteen
Re-Abort Mission

We're back where we started on page one. This is exactly how I feel about the last ten years of my life.

After I was released, I stopped for a bagel at the closest coffee shop. I got back into my car, lied down, and slept. When I woke, I couldn't even focus on the steering wheel. I was staring blankly into space. I had lost all sense of time. How long was I asleep? Did it matter? I felt like my whole life, up to this point, was all a dream and that I needed to wake up. Sadly, I knew this was my reality. These were my choices and I had to be responsible for where they had landed me.

When the whole world feels like it's crashing down on you, there are usually two ways you can go, either end it and admit defeat or press on and continue to battle this thing we call life. I chose the latter. I took a deep breath and drove myself home.

When I got there, my mother was in the bathroom vomiting.

"Dad, what's wrong with Mom?"

"I don't know. Ever since she left surgery she's been throwing up," my father answered.

I frowned, "Surgery? For what?"

"Your mother needed to get a large gallstone removed and the doctor saw something on her liver and biopsied it to test for cancer. They left the gallbladder alone, just in case."

"Jesus! Why didn't anyone tell me," I said.

"Your mother and I didn't want you to worry," As I stood there in disbelief I couldn't help think to myself, please God, don't take her from me, this can't be happening, please, I can't handle this. Somebody wake me up from this dreaded nightmare. We had to wait three weeks for those test results. I had a feeling it was going to be bad, since my mother never got sick. My father took her to the oncologist appointment. I must have called a dozen times from work asking him if they'd heard the results. Finally, my sister answered, and told me it was cancer. I ran to the bathroom and bawled. My manager happened to be in there at the same time and asked me if I needed to go home. I said yes. A coworker was kind enough to close out the rest of my tables; I somehow managed to do my cash out through my tears, ran out of there and drove home shaking. I ran inside and went straight to my mother who was sitting in my Dad's reclining chair. My two sisters and my father were there. I leaned in and hugged my mom, tears welled up in my eyes. She held onto my arm and said you have to be strong for me now. We ordered in Swiss Chalet, and all of us ate while we discussed what her next appointment would be. She was scheduled for a colonoscopy in sixty days, to find out where the cancer originated. I knew I had to go with her no matter what the cost.

    Sixty days came and went. Each day that passed was excruciating, I felt frozen, I was operating on autopilot. I couldn't eat, I couldn't sleep. My mother was vomiting all day and night. I had absolutely no expression on my face at work. People would ask me what was wrong and I would tell them to leave me alone because I couldn't talk about it. I had spent most of my years there being bullied and I certainly didn't want people like that knowing what I was going through. When we arrived at the hospital I checked my mother in at the day surgery desk. Once we got inside and she was lying down I demanded to speak to the surgeon. It had been two months since my mother had held down any food or liquid. I didn't need a medical degree to know the human body can't survive on nothing. The orderly said the doctor was too busy to come and speak to me. I said that's fine then as soon as you're finished with her I'll be wheeling her down to emerge to be treated for malnutrition and dehydration. The orderly seemed quite frazzled by that and disappeared, only to return with Doctor Mendoza who greeted us, and said that he would come out to the waiting room and speak to me immediately after my mother's procedure. I was the only one in my family that didn't take the word of medical professionals as God. I had learned firsthand there is much they know and much they don't know and I will question them as I see fit. My mother did not want me causing a fuss but I'd waited long enough. In two months, all I'd heard from the rest of my family after each doctor's appointment was that the doctors didn't seem concerned about her vomiting everything up, and her inability to eat. When he finished, he came out to see me. By then my sisters had arrived. My father was at home. He had a very bad back and it was uncomfortable for him to sit in the waiting room for hours. Dr. Mendoza seemed very kind. He told us there were tumors in the colon, nothing he thought needed to be removed, as they weren't causing blockage. He said her liver counts were not good, and there wasn't enough healthy liver to operate on to remove the liver cancer. He looked me in the eyes and said "I'm not an oncologist but to be honest I can't see them treating her. She has stage four liver cancer. I'm so sorry, but at least you have each other." I just stood there, holding back the tears. My sisters never cry and hate it when I show any emotion, so I held mine in too. I asked him why she didn't seem like herself, why was she so sick?

He leaned in close and in what I'll call a whisper said, "Sometimes when we biopsy a tumor it releases cancer into the bloodstream."

I didn't know what that meant, but due to the dirty looks my sisters were giving me I didn't dare ask. I did however ask if he could please do something to help my mother with the severe nausea and vomiting she was suffering from.

He said, "She seemed fine, actually she seemed in good spirits, and to expect her to be changing a lot over the next few months."

Then the nurse wheeled her out, and there she was, my mom was laughing and joking, she had color back in her cheeks. I could tell she was feeling much better, which didn't help my argument much, or get me any help for her condition. Of course, she was feeling better at the time they'd just given her IV, strong antinauseants, and oxygen. What was going to happen when all that wore off and she was back home?

The next period of waiting was for the oncologist appointment telling us whether they were going to treat it. My mother wouldn't let any of the doctors tell her or us how much time she had. The oncologist left the decision for treatment up to her. He said if she wanted to fight it the chances were slim; he would give it a try but the treatment would be aggressive. She said yes.

I took my mom to her first chemo appointment. She seemed okay; of course, they had the strongest shots to fight nausea there so that helped. It helped her so much she asked me to go get her a coffee and a bagel; although she didn't eat much of it. Why can't they send medication like that home with us I wondered? Half the time I was afraid to ask, or couldn't figure out who to ask, or even get my thoughts together to decide what to ask. I was in shock, and felt dead inside. My mother was sent home with what they call a baby bottle attached to her, that delivered a steady flow of chemotherapy for the next twenty-four hours until the bottle was empty. When the bottle was empty a home care nurse came, removed it, and placed it in a bio hazardous container, that we then placed under the bathroom sink. Two days in my mother got even worse, she was very weak. I was told to call the nurse from the clinic if she was experiencing any changes or discomfort. I walked in from work and my mother got up from the couch to use the washroom, I saw a blood stain where she'd been sitting. I made the call to the nurse, my mother could barely speak, I had to speak to the nurse for her. I was told to take her to the hospital immediately but my mom being the stubborn Ukrainian lady that she was wanted to wait until the morning. She slept on the couch that night while I lay awake in my bed until the sun came up. I helped my mom to the car, buckled her in, which may seem like nothing but was horrifying to me. It just made this all too real. My mother had never needed my help; she was always so strong physically and emotionally. I snapped at her to move her leg from the door, I feel awful about that, I was freaking out inside, it was like a mental state of hysteria, that just the thought of losing her put me in. It's bizarre how irrational and mean one can act toward a sick loved one, when filled with such fear, and anxiety over the reality of losing them.

I called work and said I wasn't coming in, my mom got mad at me and told me to go to work. I didn't listen, I waited until she was admitted into one of the emergency rooms, and then went to Walmart to buy her a mattress cushion to try to make it more comfortable for her. I sat at the end of her bed until midnight that night, when the doctor finally showed up to examine her. She said they would be admitting her into a room as soon as one was available. Her platelets were down and she was in danger. It also looked like the cancer had spread to her uterus. I guess that's what cancer cells being released into the bloodstream meant. The cancer had spread everywhere. I'd never understood any of those religions that won't allow surgery, up until this, for the first time it made sense to me. Cutting into my mother instantly shortened her life. She went from a perfectly functioning seventy-six-year-old, who traveled with me, went to the Casino with me, was the head manager at a very busy Tim Horton's coffee shop, into a bedridden person who couldn't even hold a conversation due to how sick she felt. The doctor had scheduled a meeting with us to deliver all the news about her condition, and what was going to be the next course of action. I slept in my mother's room the night before. My oldest sister and I were the only family members who attended that meeting. He said that there wouldn't be any more treatment, my mother's body was shutting down. In fact, he told her that she only had two weeks to live. She was devastated and fell into what seemed to be a distant depressive state. I can't imagine being told that news, and to go from being a healthy, vibrant person to being told two months later you only have two weeks to live. After she received that news her kidneys shut down over night and we were told she now had at best three to five days. After that meeting, I went back into my mother's room, and we considered each other's eyes for the last time. I hugged her, she looked so sad and defeated. She told me to go home and shower, and come back later. I never got to speak to my mom or see her in a conscious state again after that. There was only one evening when she was lying there with her eyes wide open which she shouldn't have been she was supposed to be on such a high dose of painkillers that she wouldn't be awake. I asked her to blink if she was in pain, and she did, then just to make sure I asked her to do it again, and she did. I ran out and called the nurse and asked her to give her more painkillers. The nurse had to get a doctor's approval but within minutes they gave her more and my mother seemed to be able to rest. Every night before I left, I would give strict instructions to the nurse on duty to call me any time if she awakes, or if there's any changes. That night I forgot, I thought by then everyone knew. My phone went off at four a.m. I think it was the angels telling me her time was up. I regrettably ignored it, I was exhausted. In the morning, I took my time getting ready, I wanted to shower, and get fresh clothes on, I wanted to feel human again. My sister was supposed to be picking her daughter up at the airport and dropping in first thing so I figured that gave me some time. When I was in my car on my way to see her, I got that call, the call everyone feared. My mom had passed away, with no one by her side. My sister had decided to take her daughter home first. I was pissed; I would've been there if I'd known she wasn't. When I got there, the nurse said she'd been moaning all morning, and breathing funny, which are the signs the end is coming and exactly why I'd told them to call if there were any changes. I started to question her as to why she didn't call, and then I realized it didn't matter, it was too late. I went into my mother's room and there she was. She was gone, I felt hatred for the world. I called my sister Layla, and said this is the call you've been dreading, she cried. My sister Lynn arrived, we cleaned out my mother's belongings, and went our separate ways, to our own homes. The doctor couldn't have been further off; we didn't have each other after my mom died. I didn't have anyone after my mom died. I drank vodka, cried, screamed, and started to pour my soul out to strangers on Facebook.

I found out, after all was said and done, that when a patient finds out their exact life expectancy, and they are told they don't have much time left, they go much quicker. They just lose all their fight after they hear that. I wish the doctor had never told her.

I wanted as much time as I could get with her. I could tell it was too hard for her to handle, it was too much for her mind to hear. How can anyone deal with the news that they only have two weeks to live? Someone that had just been living such a full life, at that. She slipped away mentally after that, I don't know whether it's the mind protecting itself from pain, and sadness. The mind is an extremely powerful tool. Gandhi said it best.

"A man is but the product of his thoughts; what he thinks, he becomes."

*** ***

I was a total mess. My emotions were a constant rollercoaster. One minute I'd be depressed and the next overcome with euphoria, convincing myself that everything was going to be okay. My coworkers saw this in me and instead of asking if I was all right, they picked on me even more, which didn't help at all.

    I never thought the doctors could predict the exact day my mother would pass away, but they did. They were wrong about so many things in my life. Why couldn't that be one of them? After the funeral, I swore I was not going to look back on my life and the only memories would be me crying myself to sleep every night. I prayed to God for the millionth time to please send me the love of my life, or at least a good friend. Then an idea came to me, if God won't listen then I had to create what I wanted myself. After all, God helps those who help themselves, right? What I needed most was a vacation to clear my head, reassess my goals, and hopefully find true love. With my good old trusty credit card, I decided to book a trip to Miami, Florida. I had always wanted to go there, and by God I was determined to make something good happen in my life.

Chapter Twenty
Life's A Beach

All I could hear in my head on the plane ride was my mom's voice saying, "Your phone rang, does that mean you're standing me up again?"

How many times had I chosen my friends over my mom? I had no idea. I searched my memory as hard as I could to find a number, but I couldn't, even if it was once, it was one time too many. Where are those friends now when I have no one, and need them the most?

They are unavailable.

I missed my mom so much it hurt. I wish I could see her and say sorry. Hug her and tell her how much I love her. Was I going to survive this? I was not sure of the answer to that question, not at all.

I looked out my window as we got close. I could see the blue water and the white sandy coastline. It's amazing how places you've never been to can instantly make you feel at ease, like it's home. I could feel the heat as soon as I stepped outside onto the curb. The hot sun beat down on me through my pair of coral pink Gucci sunglasses, and I knew I was in the right place.

I grabbed my suitcase outside the terminal in search of a cab. It was smoking hot. I had no idea Florida got that hot. As soon as I saw the palm trees, it felt soothing to my soul.

It didn't take long before a charming taxi driver swooped up my bags, whisked me into his cab, and onto the freeway.

"My name is Hector. Welcome to Miami," he greeted me. "Is this your first time to Miami?"

"Yes; although, I kind of feel like I've been here before," I replied.

"Ha. I know what you mean, that's how I felt when I landed here from Cuba," Hector took a cigar from a green and white box, rolled down his window and lit up, "Mind if I smoke?"

"No, not at all," I rolled down the back windows.

Normally, I would have never said yes. I hate

smoking, but I wanted to feel casual and relaxed. I felt if I gave off this type of vibe I'd attract good people in my life.

"You want to know the best thing I love about America?"

"What's that?" I said.

"Here I'll show you," he replied.

He put a CD into the player and on came the song *Purple Haze* by Jimi Hendrix.

"I have all of Jimi Hendrix's albums. American music kicks ass," said Hector.

I couldn't help but burst out laughing. Out of all the shit I've been through, here was a guy who survived escaping his home country, only to be a taxi driver in Miami, but he was making the best of it, and having a ball. If Hector could enjoy his life, why couldn't I? I considered this a very good omen. For the rest of the ride we sang along to every song that came on the radio.

When I arrived at my hotel, I tipped him a twenty-dollar bill, that may not sound like a lot, but don't forget that's twenty U.S. dollars for me. He deserved it after making my arrival so welcoming, it put me at ease and made me think I'd made the right decision by coming here.

Before I got out of the cab I realized, besides booking my hotel room, I didn't make any plans at all, I was thinking I would just be spontaneous. Since I got such a good vibe from Hector I asked him where the action was.

"The thing about Miami is, the whole beach is one big party. The way you look, I guarantee you won't have any trouble being invited to parties, the promoters will find you. Adios," said Hector, waving goodbye and driving off into the distance.

Once inside my room, I plopped myself onto the bed. My eyes were instantly drawn to an art deco painting hanging on the wall. It was a picture of an elegant couple on a staircase, holding hands and looking toward the ocean during a moonlit summer night as various couples slow danced beneath them. They reminded me of my parents, two people that loved each other until the very end. Maybe this was another good sign that my wish of finding true love would finally become a reality while I was here. Wasting no time, I jumped into the shower, shaved, changed into my bikini, and ran out to the beach.

As I walked down Ocean Drive, I realized that Hector wasn't exaggerating. The long weekend had just begun and the streets were packed with people, cars, trucks, SUVs, and buses with video screens on the side cruising up and down Ocean Drive and Washington St., pumping out the music that they were promoting. The party had begun and it was still day light. After walking over one city block, I did a double take. Here I was, trying to be more grounded and all I could see was bling everywhere; designer clothes, diamond jewelry, fancy cars, hip-hop artists, and ballers. I realized being around wealthy sports players made me want that luxurious lifestyle.

As I looked at my reflection in a storefront window, I decided I deserved to have the life I wanted because I was a good person. The idea of being rich and having the financial security that guaranteed I would have a roof over my head for the rest of my life, would be deeply satisfying to me. It would give me the freedom to pursue my other dreams of being in the movie business and traveling the world.

They say, money can't buy happiness but it sure could buy me the chance to produce my own film, and that would make me happy. Even though I didn't have any money to spend on clothes, I went inside the store, I had to. I was in Fashion Heaven; every single dress was sparkling with crystals, and bright in color. I felt so out of place in my ripped jeans. It's not a crime to want beautiful things. I walked over to the dress rack and found a dress covered in Swarovski crystals, it twinkled like diamonds. I tried to find a price tag, but none of the clothing had prices on them.

"Excuse me Miss. Where are the price tags? Could you tell me how much this dress is?" I asked the sales woman.

She looked at me like I was a moron.

"This is Ocean Drive. None of the clothing has price tags," she replied in a snotty Spanish accent.

Without stooping to her level, I decided to deal with a different sales person.

"Excuse me, do you know what the price of this is?" I asked the young blonde.

She smiled, "That's a beautiful dress. Why don't you try it on?"

I knew this game; they try to get you in the changing room so they can guilt you into buying something whether you can afford it or not. They even offered me a glass of champagne, followed by a shot of vodka. I gratefully turned down both. Who knows what damage I could do in a drunken state of mind?

Then they force you to come out of the changing room to see yourself in the dress, by putting the only mirrors in the middle of the store.

"Wow! You look amazing in that dress," said the blonde.

I looked in the mirror and saw what I always wanted to be; a successful, happy woman in beautiful clothing. It was as if I had been transformed into a different person the second I put this dress on. I didn't feel like a loser. I felt like a winner. The sales woman wasn't bullshitting, I looked drop dead gorgeous in this outfit. It hugged my curves in all the right places.

"How much is it?" I asked.

"That one is one thousand five hundred dollars," she said.

My mouth dropped.

There was no way I could afford that dress, no matter how badly I wanted it. I still had bills waiting for me back home, plus hotel expenses to pay while I was there.

"I was wondering if you would do me a favor? Can you take a picture of me in the dress?" I asked.

"Well, normally it's against our policy, but sure, no problem," I passed her my cell phone, and she snapped a few shots of me.

I figured if I couldn't have the dress, at least I could have the memory of me in it to motivate me in life. I took one quick photo of all the bling'd out dresses while the sales staff weren't looking then changed back into my jeans and wandered outside.

Groups of rowdy guys wandered the streets alongside me. Every other minute, guys would grab at me or started yelling offensive sexual remarks. I was called snowflake, blondie, old school Britney Spears (I'm not even sure what that means). I felt so uncomfortable. The way they were staring at me and trying to hit on me wasn't even flattering, it was perverted. I had several men ask me if I wanted to be with the whole group of them. Gross. Just when I thought I made it through the chaos, five new guys pulled up in front of me in their SUV convertible, driving slow. They each had on a different colored polo, with denim shorts, and looked like a bunch of underage prep boys.

The guy in the passenger seat leaned out of his window and yelled, "Hey baby! Can I buy you a sex on the beach?"

All his friends high fived each other.

I ignored them and started walking faster toward my hotel. Passenger seat guy jumped out of the car and started following me, yelling for me to slow down.

It was a crowded street, no one could have heard my cries or would have cared if he pulled me into an alley and had his way with me. I started to panic and sped up even more.

When I turned around, trying to check if I lost him, the guy grabbed a hold of me and pulled me into him. He tried to give me a kiss.

Judging by the whiskey on his breath, he was wasted.

"Let go of me," I yelled.

No one in the crowd even flinched.

"Come on, bitch. I just want to buy you a drink," I gasped and tried to punch him, but he grabbed my arm.

"Calm the fuck down. Let's just you and I go back to my place," he said.

"Somebody help me," I yelled.

For all I knew, he was going to rape me. I had never been so fearful in a crowded place in all my life. Just when I was going to try and knee him in the balls, a six foot two young man in his late twenties with a slim build and a beautiful smile, came out of nowhere. What struck me right away was his southern accent and his perfect teeth.

"You heard the girl, let her go," said the southern gentlemen.

"Piss off," said the passenger seat guy, as he raised his arm to punch my knight in shining armor. He put the drunk in a choke hold, I could hear a crunching sound.

"Next time treat a girl with respect. Now run home

to your mommy before I bust you up," The drunk guy jumped back into his car with his friends, and they sped off.

"That was awesome! Thank you for rescuing me," I said.

He introduced himself to me and ironically, his name was Nicholas, Nick for short. Here we go Nick number two is up to bat. As I'm checking him out I noticed he was trying to hide his diamond jewelry, he had a huge diamond cuff on his wrist, and a diamond chain with a diamond cross around his neck. We stood on the street talking for over an hour. I was finally having a sober compelling interaction with a man. We were having an actual conversation. It wasn't awkward, I wasn't nervous. He was funny, smart, and super cute, with a great personality. He was American, but his background was half Irish, and half Jamaican.

After an hour of talking I told him up front, "I'm going to be straight up with you Nick. Don't even bother trying to come back to my room," I said.

"I have a million-dollar house up the beach, I don't need your room Lily," he said in his sexy southern Atlanta accent.

"Yeah, I've heard that one before," I said.

"So where are your friends at," asked Nick.

I didn't want to answer, it's weird to travel alone, I knew that. I didn't have a choice. It was either being alone at home sitting in my room crying nonstop over my mother, or try to go on. I needed a vacation to clear my head, and get myself back together. I was going to do my best to enjoy Miami and whatever adventure came my way. Nicholas tilted his head down and looked at me through the top of his sunglasses. There was something unique about him. His mannerisms, his facial expressions, that southern accent, and the way he kept repeating my name with it. Ahh Nick!

"Okay you got me, I'm here alone but I…"

Nick's cell phone went off.

"Yeah. Where you at? Uh-huh. Uh-huh. Right, I'll be there in minute," said Nick.

"Who was that, your girlfriend?" I asked.

"Funny girl, Nah, that's my boy, he says they want to go to a club. You want to come. My car is just down the street. Up to you Lily," I knew it was risky to run off with a random stranger like this but Nicholas seemed different, he was attractive, funny, and made me feel like it was okay to be myself.

Of course, I said yes, I would have been dumb not to. As we walked down the block we passed by a Bentley. I imagined how one day I would be able to buy myself a car like that.

I continued down the block when Nick shouted, "Yo Lily! Where you going?"

"This is your car?" I asked.

"Ya, hop in," Nick replied as if having a Bentley was nothing.

I should have known; the color of the car was violet blue with a silver front grill and silver rims. This car suited Nick's style to a T. I got in the car and off we went.

Inside the interior, the leather seat cushions were white with little holes in them and violet blue contours around the edges. I started wondering what he did for a living but felt it best to keep it to myself for now, I didn't want to ruin the moment that was happening between us.

"Nick, do you mind dropping me off at my hotel? I need to go to my room and get changed."

"No problem Lily, I got you."

He waited for me out front. I put on my gold paisley dress with gold sequins around the hips and wore it with my gold strappy heels. When I came down we got in the car and he started driving out of South Beach then he got on the highway. Fuck. Where the hell was he taking me, I thought.

He must have read my mind because the next words out of his mouth were, "Don't worry I'm not going to chop you up into little pieces, if that's what you're afraid of."

"Well thank God for that," I said with an uneasy laugh.

"You're not a cop are you," asked Nick.

"No, why?" I replied.

"Because if I ask you have to tell me," answered Nick.

Obviously, I started to think he did things that were illegal.

"Mind if I ask you something Nick?" I said.

"What?" said Nick.

"What is it that you do for a living?" I asked.

"Not now Lily, first let's get a few drinks then I'll tell you before the nights over, I promise," said Nick.

When we arrived at the club, I met a couple of his friends, had a few drinks, we both decided we were starving and then took off to an IHOP pancake restaurant. Just before getting into the car we stood outside for a minute, he put his arms around me, then said to his friend,

"Don't we make a perfect couple," My heart almost stopped, he sounded so sincere, but I knew I was not a good judge of character, and couldn't tell if he meant it. At the restaurant, we talked for hours. He told me about his life growing up in the hood in Atlanta then a story about meeting a certain baseball player. You guessed it, Mark. I couldn't believe it! Out of all the athletes in the world he could've met and had a story about, there he was sitting across from me talking about Mark. Of course, I pretended I didn't know who he was talking about. After our long conversation, I was even more interested in Nick, and even more attracted to him, I didn't want to ruin it by admitting I knew a ball player. When the clock struck eight a.m., I excused myself to the bathroom and looked at myself in the mirror. I had dark circles under my eyes, and looked like crap, splashing water on my face did nothing, I had expired, I needed to go to bed. I learned the meaning of beauty sleep at that moment.

"I had an amazing time Nick, but I'm from Canada and I don't pull all-nighters. I need to go back to my hotel, and get some sleep," I said.

Nick immediately signaled for the waitress to bring the bill, paid for everything and we walked back to his car. Once inside we sat there for a moment looking deep into each other's eyes. He was playing the new Jamie Foxx song, "DJ Play a Love Song,"

"What are you thinking Lily?"

I didn't want to tell him what I was thinking, it was crazy. I had this amazing feeling in my stomach that I was about to fall in love. I was sitting there silently praying this moment would never end, wishing I could freeze this moment in time and replay it over and over and never have to search for that special someone ever again. I was feeling and hoping this was it, I'd finally found my soul mate. I couldn't tell him that! He'd run for the hills. "I can't tell you, it's stupid," I said. How could I tell this guy I'd just met that I somehow knew I could fall in love with him and spend the rest of my life with him. That would be weird. The second I said it, all this would be over. "Just tell me what you're thinking and maybe it will come true," said Nick. I converted my true feelings into a more acceptable answer and said, "I wish we could hang out, go jet skiing and spend the rest of my vacation together."

"Why can't we? If that's what you want, then that's what we'll do."

I wanted to believe him, so I did. My interest and my attraction for him had grown with every hour we spent together and we hadn't even kissed yet. I had to pursue this to see what could come of it. However as much as I was taken by this man's charm I couldn't stay awake one minute longer.

"You want to come back to my place instead?" he asked.

"Do you really have a million-dollar mansion?" I said.

"Come over and find out," said Nick.

Considering the cost of his fancy car, my curiosity got the best of me. I wanted to see if this million-dollar house up the beach existed, so I said yes.

We headed onto the highway out of Miami toward Fort Lauderdale. Nick pulled up to a security gate, punched in his code and parked in front of his mansion. I couldn't believe this was happening to me. His place was gorgeous, all four stories of it. The entire place was surrounded by 12-foot floor-to-ceiling glass windows providing incredible panoramic views of the bay and the Miami skyline in the distance. He also had a BMW and a Mercedes parked in his drive way but I still didn't know what he did for a living. We got out of the car, and just before we entered the house he said, "Just a minute."

I asked, "What," as he brushed my bangs aside he looked deep into my eyes. "There's something I've been wanting to do since I met you," He leaned over and kissed me on the lips. I think I blacked out for a minute, that's how good it felt. It was gentle, soft, tender, and meaningful.

I instantly knew I was in danger of losing myself in this man. I said we're just going inside to cuddle, and sleep, right? That's it, right? This line never worked, I don't know why I even bothered using it, but I did. Nick was a total gentleman. He even lent me a white cotton t-shirt. I changed, crawled under the covers and passed out within seconds.

My alarm clock was the Miami sun glaring through the glass windows. As beautiful as it was I could have used a bit more sleep. I was exhausted and was up before him. Not wanting to be alone I carefully nudged him awake. We started to kiss. The kissing turned into touching, which turned into us spending the next 48 hours in his bedroom. This was the most powerful connection I'd ever had, which is hard to believe considering the strong feelings I'd felt for all the men in my past. I was so comfortable staring directly into his eyes while we made love. Our kisses would move from the lips, to the cheek down to my neck back up the side of my face and onto my lips. Our bodies moved so in sync and effortlessly from one position to another.

He whispered in my ear, "Did you think it would feel like this? You make me never want to leave this room."

I thought fuck no, I didn't think it would feel this

amazing. I'd had great moments with my ex-boyfriends but this was a whole new level of intimacy and passion I didn't even know existed. I wished with every cell in my body that this moment would never end because I was feeling and thinking everything that he was whispering in my ear which made each moment even more passionate and more intense. We would sleep cuddling, shower together, order in food, then go back to bed for more. It was like a fairy sprinkled fairy dust on us. It was as if he could read my mind, and knew exactly what I liked, and needed. I truly felt like I'd found my soul mate. The way he looked at me made me feel like we were falling in love. The way he kissed me, and held me, felt incredible. Everything was perfect, passionate, and comfortable. I never considered anyone's eyes and felt like that. Such an intense closeness so fast I never dreamed could happen to me. When I looked in his eyes, it was like I'd known him my whole life. I always relied on alcohol to be with someone when I was single to numb my guilt and lower my inhibitions. I am too shy when I'm sober. That wasn't the case with Nick.

After two days of love making even our shower together was intimate. He took a wash cloth and washed my face and my entire body so gently always maintaining eye contact like he was lost in love as he gazed into my eyes. I don't want to ever forget the way he looked at me, I felt so special.

"Lily, if you could do anything today what would it be?" asked Nick.

"Have you show me around Miami, spend the day together, swim, lie in the sun, cuddle on the beach."

"Anything for you Lily," said Nick.

He drove us to a farmer's market. Out of all the places he could have taken me I thought it was a poor choice until I arrived. I immediately was drawn to a fabulous juice bar that had all the healthy smoothies, and fresh green juices that I need, and have grown to love due to their many health, and skin benefits. They had organic greens, fruits, and a huge list of supplements that are great for your skin, and for someone with fibro. This may not sound like a big deal but for someone who was aging, and dealing with chronic pain, it was a life saver. Miami quickly became my new second home.

After a quick bite to eat we decided to browse around the stores on Ocean Drive. When we got to the dress store I had visited a few days ago, I couldn't resist going back in to check out that dress one last time. When we got inside the sales girl didn't recognize me from before, which was a relief.

"You like these dresses don't you Lily" said Nick.

"Yes. I think they're beautiful".

"Try one on, you must've dragged me in here for a reason," Nick said with that million-dollar smile he had.

He knew me so well it was hard to believe we'd just met. I didn't hesitate, I went straight for the dress I fell in love with the first time I was in there. When I came out of the change room Nick looked shocked.

"Damn, Lily. You look so beautiful."

"Thanks, I tried it on before but…. any way maybe someday I'll be able to buy it," I said.

"How much is it," asked Nick.

"It doesn't matter, let's just go, I just wanted you to see how pretty it looked," I replied.

Nick asked the sales guy how much it was, he said two thousand, and Nick took out the cash from his pocket and paid for the dress.

"No way. I can't let you do that. I didn't bring you here to get you to buy me the dress, honestly," I said.

"Don't worry, you should have it, but only on one condition," he said.

"What's that?" I inquired.

Nick got up and passed me a pair of matching high heels.

"Excuse me, how much for the shoes?" asked Nick.

"Those are five hundred dollars," replied the sales clerk.

"Try these on with the dress," said Nick.

I slipped on the heels and looked in the mirror. I felt like a princess.

"Lily, now you look like you belong in South Beach.

"We'll take them too," said Nick.

I couldn't believe this was happening. Everything was so perfect, it made me nervous. I gave Nick a big kiss, and hug then we took off in his Bentley.

"Lily, there is some business I have to take care of. I'll drop you off at your hotel and pick you up later tonight. We'll go to Club Bed, and you can wear your new dress," said Nick.

I gave him a kiss on the lips, he gave me his cell number and I jumped out of the car feeling like I was on cloud nine.

I went to my room, had a shower, got into my bikini and went to the beach. By the time I got back to my room, it was after six in the evening. There was not a single message on my phone. I checked the voicemail for my room but there was none. Worry started to fill my head and my stomach, I felt sick. Was he hurt? Maybe he lost my number, and he didn't know my last name which means he couldn't reach me at the hotel? Did I do something wrong? I stayed up all night sitting in my room waiting for his call but nothing came. I called his cell phone, it went directly to voicemail so I hung up. God damn it, why does this keep happening to me. Why couldn't Nick be the one. Why isn't he answering? Once again only I felt a connection and the guy was just faking it? Really?

I passed out at four in the morning with my phone in my hand, how pathetic is that.

The following day nothing changed. I still had not heard from Nick in over twenty-four hours. Instead of enjoying my trip I was obsessing about a guy who wasn't calling. Was I being naïve in believing he felt something special too? Then I thought to myself why would a guy drop over two thousand dollars on a girl he didn't care about? The whole thing just didn't make sense. After sitting at the pool sipping rum punch all day I remembered tomorrow was my last night in Miami before going home. I couldn't stand the thought of never seeing Nick again so I did the only thing I could think of. I left Nick a voice mail stating when I was leaving and that I would like to see him on my last night before I left. A few minutes later my phone rang.

"Nick. Where have you been? Are you okay?" I asked.

"I'm fine" he replied.

"You have some nerve you know; I've been waiting for your call for over two days" I said.

"I know, I'm sorry, really I am. Lily, there's something I need to discuss with you, it's important" said Nick.

"What is it? You can tell me", I said.

"No not on the phone. This needs to be done face to face."

We agreed to meet at a bar in South Beach. I arrived early and Nick walked in twenty minutes later. We sat in a booth close to the bar. He didn't bother with small talk. He got straight to the point.

"So how do you like Miami?"

"I love it! I'd move here in an instant if I could."

"Lily, what if I could make that happen," he asked.

"The only way I could do that is if I married you so I could get a green card. I somehow doubt that's what you want," I laughed.

"No, you wouldn't have to marry me, I could get you in another way."

"How?"

"Before I answer that, there's something I've been meaning to tell you. The truth is; during these past two days, I've been doing a lot of thinking. That's why I didn't call you back."

"You spent two days thinking, this must be serious," I said.

"It is. I'm not going to lie; when I first met you, and looked in to your eyes, I felt like I could trust you. You've been on my mind ever since I saw you. Please tell me I can trust you."

He stared deeply into my eyes.

This was it, I thought, the day I'd dreamt about my whole life, it was here. My true love was staring right at me about to confess his love with all his heart.

"Well, aren't you going to answer me?"

I smiled, "Yes Nick. You can trust me, in fact you'll never meet a more genuine person, now what did you want to tell me? What's going on?"

"You mean it? Lily, you once asked me what I do for a living and I'm ready to tell you."

"It's okay Nick. You can tell me," I replied.

"Alright, my Dad and his partner are in jail for a con and my father always told me that the most important thing is to pick a partner who truly loves you, that way they won't give you up if they get arrested. Do you think you could survive in prison, I mean, I would hire the best lawyers to get you out?"

I went into shock, but I played it cool by simply answering, "No Nick, I don't think I'd do well in jail, I'm a wimp and I don't want to lick anyone's pussy."

Nick scoped the place before responding, "See that girl over there?"

I looked at the direction he was pointing. An attractive black female with long hair and tight clothing was chatting up an older businessman in an expensive suit.

"That's one of my girls."

"So, you're a pimp then?"

"Not exactly, you see one of my hustles is to get hot women, like Charlene, to stake out high end hotels in Miami, their job is to flirt with rich businessmen in town, the ones with Rolex's, diamond rings, hopefully carrying some cash. Charlene gets invited back to their room, roofies them and robs them. You have to be able to assess their height and weight so you'll know how much to give them in order not to kill them."

Nick was explaining this very business-like. I had to give him credit, he had done well for himself at such a young age, luxury cars, a mansion in Miami, diamond jewelry, designer clothes from head to toe, wow, but that was not the life for me.

I instantly felt sick to my stomach.

"I also figured out a way to convince rich, retired seniors to invest in some property that isn't real and that con can get us millions. But that's all I'm saying; I need to know you're joining the business before I tell you anymore."

"Hold on a minute, why would I need to worry about getting arrested," I asked.

"I know a guy that can get you papers so you can move here with no hassle, but if you decide to move to Miami, I need you to be part of my business."

"What about Charlene?" I asked.

"I have lots of women working for me."

I couldn't believe what I was hearing.

"Lily, I don't plan on doing this forever. I just need a big enough bank roll to start an empire like Trump. You're not getting any younger, you should make a move now, no more bills to worry about. No more working shitty jobs, making shitty money. They say money isn't everything but I'm telling you, once you get it, you enjoy it, trust me, this is Miami baby! So, Lily, what do you think,"

Nick asked.

I looked over at Charlene as she escorted the executive outside the bar. This is it, the million-dollar question. Do I sacrifice my ethics to chase my dream of finding true love and settling down in a city that I adore or should I do the right thing? I had never smoked before but for once in my life, I somehow needed one right then and there. I asked a guy beside me for a cigarette and lit it up.

"Nick, you're gonna have to give me a minute. Once I finish this smoke, I will give you my answer. I pressed the cigarette to my lips and slowly exhaled. The raw taste of tobacco was nauseating, but did provide a quick sense of calm. I knew this would be the last time I'd ever smoke a cigarette and depending on how I played this situation, quite possibly the last time I'd ever see Nick. We both sat there, almost suspended in time, not moving a muscle; except for, swallowing down my vodka and Coke. The cigarette was nearly done.

What should I do?

How badly did I want this?

My exhale was the only sound that registered in my mind. When it came to the final drag, I butt it out in the ashtray, chugged the rest of my drink and said, "Nick, I'm sorry. I can't take people's money. If you want to take money from each of those ball players that treat women like shit, I'm down, but my parents brought me up to be a good, honest person. I can't be a criminal. It's just not in me."

"Lily, I wish I met you when we were younger."

I'm not sure what that meant. I'm guessing he thought that naïve, twenty-year-old Lily would've believed she was the love of his life and all this was just for them to build a life together, but I was beyond that. I was smarter than that.

I kissed him goodbye, and left the bar, never looking back.

CHAPTER TWENTY-ONE
Last Call

My fantasy was over.

What is it that stops guys from falling for me?

Do I snore like a wild beast?

Am I farting in my sleep?

There was this one time my date sat me down and said he had something serious he needed to talk to me about. Turns out, I had let one rip on his leg when I fell asleep. He asked me if that was going to be a problem after it happened two nights in a row. It wasn't a problem for me.

Geez, doesn't everyone fart?

Truthfully, when Nick asked me if I was a cop, I chose to ignore it. I didn't want to walk away from him that night. I didn't want to go back to my room and be all alone again. It took every ounce of strength I had to accept that our moment together was over, because being with him felt so good.

I'm a joke.

My dream guy turned out to be a criminal. I was conned; yet, there is still a part of me that believes his feelings were genuine.

I walked over to the nearest convenience store and bought a bottle of Grey Goose. I needed something to numb my despair and disappointment.

I took my bottle of vodka and sat down in the sand with the beautiful blue ocean in front of me and the fake glow from the neon signs behind me.

As I sat there drinking, feeling sorry for myself, the clouds rolled in, some were pink, the rest were various shades of purple and blue.

It was like a painting. Everything felt so surreal.

After finishing off the bottle, I realized that sitting on the beach alone wasn't helping, so I wandered into the first bar I saw. I didn't care what it looked like, I just needed to be around people.

As I stepped inside, I noticed the bar was empty, I grabbed a stool anyway, and ordered a Cosmo. The bartender and waitress, who were both in their late thirties, were talking to each other about what they were going to do after work. They both mentioned something to do with their husband and wife.

"Excuse me. I don't mean to interrupt, but I couldn't help but overhear your conversation. I have a question for ya," I said.

They both turned toward me.

"Sure, what is it?" asked the male bartender.

"What's it like? You know, marriage?"

"It's good, but it's work. I had to make a lot of compromises. It can get dull but so can hanging out in bars. We see a lot of crazy stuff here on the beach. I don't miss that scene at all," he said.

"How about you? What's your take on this?" I aggressively asked the waitress.

"Sometimes, I miss the feeling you get when you make out with someone new, you know the butterflies in your stomach, that raw passion, the throw down. After a few years, all that starts to fade. Sometimes I feel like we're roommates, rather than lovers, stay single, have fun," she said.

"It's not fun being deceived. Most casual sex involves deception, or at the very least a feeling of disappointment when you have great chemistry and he doesn't even give it a chance to see if it could be more. I can't separate intimacy from my emotions," was my reply to her advice.

"If you ask me, the word *love* loses all meaning after a while. As you get older, you start to realize that you need to settle down, sometimes fate makes the decision of who you do that with," he said.

"What you're telling me is that you settled?" I asked.

"Doesn't everyone?"

"I don't know if I agree with that," said the female bartender, "Not everyone gets married because it's time. Some people experience love at first sight and stay in love throughout their lives together."

"That's bullshit. Instant attraction is not love, that's called lust. True love is when you know you will be by that person's side no matter what comes your way. The problem with today's society is that people have become disposable like their morning coffee cup. Hollywood romance doesn't exist, even celebrities don't last forever," said the male bartender.

As I sat there listening to both perspectives, I started to feel angry so I paid for my drink and got up to leave.

Before I reached the door, I turned around and said, "You're wrong. Just because you settled doesn't mean everyone does. Love at first sight does exist. It's a feeling that can only be understood by people who have felt it. Love can last a lifetime and still mean something, true love does exist, I've seen it, and it's the most powerful gift you could experience here on earth."

I stormed out of the bar and called it a night.

The next day, I packed up my things, grabbed a cab, and went to the airport.

As I sat there, waiting for my flight, I thought about all my adventures.

I have to believe that one day I'll find that special someone, when the moment is right. Otherwise the bitterness of not having the life I want will consume me, and repel any friendship or love that comes my way. This isn't the life I saw for myself but my anger about it is making my life worse. Going back to Toronto without the man of my dreams wasn't such a big deal after all, I learned a lot about myself. I still had the will to fall in love. I had to accept finding true love must have no time line. If I was open to the possibility I already had the most amazing gift of all, hope. When things get rough or lonely I must keep my faith alive, stay positive, nothing in the world can stop me if I'm radiating a positive energy. I will keep my heart open and keep chasing my dreams.

With love,

Lily Monroe

About The Author

"I grew up in a few towns and cities in Ontario, Canada. I think that makes me a hybrid. I'm small-town city girl. After my sister's daughter started dating she fell into the same unhealthy patterns of falling for players as I had. My sister would call me for advice frequently, and to my surprise all the experiences I had made me quite an expert on how to detect player behavior and when to walk away. At the time, I was pursuing acting and waitressing so in turn I would call her to vent about my ridiculous day serving the dysfunctional public. After six years of her harassing me to write a book, because I had great advice and funny stories, I decided to pour my heart into a novel and give my sister's ear a rest. My book turned into a story about a young woman dealing with two decades of being single and searching for love, she survives those twenty years by living in the moment. Some of the moments were to escape chronic pain, sometimes loneliness, and toward the end, it was to deal with grief. There were nights in Miami with shady men, famous athletes, even a private eye. In this life journey, I dealt with illness, jealousy, judgment, adult bullying, grief, all while trying to survive and find a purpose to this life of solitude I kept finding myself in."

DEDICATIONS

To you, all of you who have a heart that's beating and starving for love. Even if you have self-love you still need human interaction, and friendship.

To my sister, because this wouldn't even exist if you hadn't spent years demanding me to write.

To my niece, Rebecca, it was the closeness of the three of us that helped me discover my experiences could benefit others.

To the men who shared passionate moments with me, they are some of my favorite memories.

To Ja'kel, my publisher, you were the missing piece of this puzzle that helped me get a final draft I'm proud to share.

www.ingramcontent.com/pod-product-compliance
Lightning Source LLC
Chambersburg PA
CBHW030902080526
44589CB00010B/109